Has God Spoken?

by

A.O. SCHNABEL

Revised
and
Enlarged

CREATION-LIFE PUBLISHERS
San Diego, Ca. 92115

Library of Congress #74-81483

ISBN 0-89051-009-1

Copyright © 1974
CREATION-LIFE PUBLISHERS
San Diego, California

TABLE OF CONTENTS

FOREWORD

A knowledge of the evidences of Christianity is essential to each of God's children. Without knowledge of the reasonable credentials of the Gospel, our faith will lack conviction and reality, and our ministry will not carry the necessary zeal and diligence. As small children we accept unquestioningly our parent's faith, as does the young Jewish and Hindu child. Now our God demands that we be ready always to give answer to the unbeliever that asks us a reason concerning our hope of eternal life (I Peter 3:15).

Too few Christians realize the burden of proof falls upon the one who states, "There is a God and the Bible is His revelation of Himself to us." The denial of the unbelievers cannot be proved, but in reality the challenge is for the believer to "prove his statement". God has not handicapped this generation, but has given us ample evidence of His existence, His nature, and that He has spoken to us through men in the past. The purpose of this study therefore is to accredit the testimony of the writers of the Bible. A person's faith can be founded on the fact that their written record is a reliable and faithful witness, both historically and scientifically. The integrity of the Bible stands on the proven integrity of its writers.

INTRODUCTION

IF there is a God who is supreme over our universe, and IF the Bible is the revelation from that God, then there is ONE essential that must be inherent within that revelation. It must be constituted solely of TRUTHS! It is an absolute necessity then, that statements of Bible writers, when describing or mentioning physical laws of this universe, other than allowances for poetic license, must coincide perfectly with all known facts of science (not necessarily theories). Furthermore, they must do this regardless of the accepted theories and level of scientific knowledge of the age in which they were written.

This work has been written to demonstrate that between the observations of science and a simple, direct interpretation of the Bible narrative there exists a harmony such as would be expected of a book having the same Author as the physical world.

If you, the reader, can be shown proof of the above statement, then truly you have seen beyond any doubt a miracle in this scientific age as unexplainable as any recorded in the Bible. It is beyond comprehension that men who lived 2000 to 4000 years ago could, without this age's scientific instruments, arrive at the same knowledge as the men of science have in the last three hundred years.

Modern instruments in the research field represent our greatest advancement in science. So it is machine technology that allows us to broaden our knowledge beyond that of our forefathers.

Leeuwenhoek's invention of the microscope in 1676; the use of shock waves in the study of the ocean floor; the operation in November of 1963 of the world's largest radio telescope, these and countless other tools have recorded in the scientific journals of our day discoveries of this universe's secrets that otherwise would be impossible for the unaided human mind to search out.

As evidence of their Divine Guidance the writers of the Bible have included scientific truths in non-scientific terms. Truths that for centuries the skeptics considered as errors because it disagreed with their darkened understanding. Truths that have come to light in recent times only through painstaking and costly research. Truths that without the later development of instruments would have been impossible for us to witness with our own eyes as facts.

Moreover a study of the Bible in this age, where science and materialism have become common idols, shows no reflection of scientific error. This is the second half of our miracle. Thus not only does this book predescribe later scientific discoveries, but it does so without allowing entrance of any error that was believed in the age in which it was written.

IS God the unseen author of the Bible? Let us create a simple parallel problem of ownership. We could tell of an old magnificent home that had stood unclaimed as long as any local resident could remember. One day a man came to the town and claimed the house to be his. Since no records existed either in writing or in any resident's memory, many disputed his claim. To verify his ownership, the man said he had been the builder and would offer as evidence to this fact some of the house's internal construction secrets. He told of a cement trowel that had fallen into the wet cement foundation and was entombed at one corner; of hidden floor joists that were made of 2x8's instead of the standard 2x6's; and over two dozen more unseen facts of the interior construction. If the house was torn open enough to reveal these secrets, would you as the local judge declare this house to be his, based on this evidence? Scientists have torn open the universe and uncovered it's construction secrets. Let us compare these with statements from the pre-scientific age book that claims to be from the same builder: Jehovah.

The question confronting us now is by what means did those ancient writers, none of whom could be considered scientists or to have had adequate instruments, acquire an amazingly accurate knowledge of certain major discoveries of the last three centuries? This study is intended to bring to your attention the "facts" in their writings. The answer to the question — by what means? — is for you, the reader, to ponder.

Our method of study will be to first read and analyze an ancient Bible writer's statement of fact, then look at man's historical record (in chronological order) of knowledge pertaining to that fact. The reader should note that all dates used are only approximate as determined by reliable authorities. The New American Standard Bible, printed in 1960, is used because of its modern language and its well known textual accuracy.

I
Astronomy

Astronomy is one of the oldest sciences in man's history. Paradoxically, little truth was known of our universe until the 20th century as is evident in the following study. To begin this comparative study in astronomy, let us consider a few basic facts concerning this planet we live on.

1. THE EARTH IS SPHERICAL

Bible Writers: 1033-975 B.C.
Solomon wrote in Proverbs 8:27, "He inscribed a circle on the face of the deep."

745-695 B.C.
Isaiah 40:22, "It is He that sitteth above the circle of the earth."

ANALYSIS: The Hebrew word "Khug" is translated "circle". A more exact connotation would be "sphericity" or "roundness". The use of the word "deep" refers to the deep bodies of water, similar to our word "depth". The Hebrew word "erets" for "earth" is used in two senses by the ancient writers. One use denotes the entire world, while the more common usage was limited to only the dry land portion as used in Genesis 1:10.

FACT: The earth was known to be "rounded" or "spherical" including the ocean face or water lines.

History of Science: 384-322 B.C.

In every civilization, other than Israel, the unearthed records show man taught the earth to be flat. The first arguments set forth for a spherical earth were by the famous Greek, Aristotle. These were: ships disappear over the horizon, and the circular shape seen on the moon during an eclipse of the latter. Disappointingly few people, other than Aristotle's personal students, were convinced by this evidence.

200 B.C.

When the Romans became the world rulers they "did not continue the scientific attitude of the Greeks . . . They returned to the disk shaped earth of the early Greeks, and the Roman 'Orbis Terrarum' became the standard of the world for 13 centuries."[1]

1520 A.D.

The common man held the earth was flat until "the introduction of the compass and improved sailing vessels made possible the voyages of Columbus, Magellan, and others. These great discoveries caused a revolution in map making"[2] which finally brought general acceptance of the fact that the earth is spherical.

1800 A.D.

"At the end of the 17th century, the sextant, telescope, theodolite, the planetable, the barometer, and accurate pendulum clocks were available for land measurements."[3]

---

[1] Erwin Raisz, "Map", Encyclopedia Americana, Vol. 18, 1957 ed. p. 258a.

[2] Same as above note, IBID

[3] Same as above note, IBID

2. THE EARTH REVOLVES DAILY

Bible Writers: 2000 B.C.
Job 38:12-14a, "Have you ever in your life commanded the morning, and caused the dawn to know its place; . . . It is changed like clay under the seal."

1015 B.C.
Maschil's Psalm speaking of King David, Psalms 89:36, 37
"His descendants shall endure forever,
And his throne as the sun before me.
It shall be established forever like the moon,
And the witness in the sky is faithful."

ANALYSIS: The Hebrew word "changed" in Job 38:14 carries the meaning "changed by turning". "Seals" were commonly used as signature rings in ancient days. Today's museums show they generally were constructed of an engraved round semiprecious stone mounted on a ring. The engraved stone, called a signate, would be pressed into damp clay, then the clay turned to make an impression of concentric circles. Each man's ring contained a stone of different shape, and therefore became his personal and unmistakable signature. Thousands of variations were possible as with today's flat key. The sun's apparent motion at daybreak as appears to an observer on earth is explained by example. Job paralleled the break-of-day to the impression left by the signate ring in the clay.
Note the following comparison in Fig. 1.
Thus God's instruction to Job is: The ring (sun) which makes the impression (daybreak) is held in a fixed position and the clay (earth) which receives the impression (daybreak) is rotated completely around so

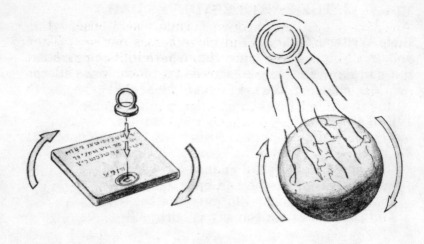

Fig. 1

that the ring (sun) appears in its original position once again.

Hebrew poetry is composed of two parallel verses that have a direct relationship to each other. The second verse usually expressing the same thought as the first, only in different words. Thus, Maschil calls the moon "the faithful witness in the sky". The moon has always witnessed to man that which it observes and man can not, namely sunlight after sunset. The one thing the moon tells us, is the location of the sun at night.

FACT: Job wrote that the sun which appears at daybreak and seems to move through our sky, is actually stationary. Instead, it is our earth beneath the sun that is rotating. The psalm writer, Maschil, recorded that the moon witnessed, through reflection, the sun's position to man at night.

History of Science: 384-322 B.C.

Ancient civilizations through normal visual observation concluded that the sun did move across our sky. They conjectured many theories as to where it disappeared at night, and how it reappeared the next day at the opposite side of the sky. The idea that the earth revolves around the sun as a body in the solar system was ventured as a hypothesis by Aristotle.

146-1543 A.D.

Contrary to the earlier theory of Aristotle, Claudius Ptolemy devised a planetary system that was accepted until the 16th century. He theorized that there was an immovable earth at the center of the universe with a "primum mobile", that carried all the celestial bodies, and rotated once a day around the earth.

1543 A.D.

The Copernicus System, published in 1543 by Nicolaus Copernicus, explained the apparent motion of the heavenly bodies as due to the earth's daily rotation and annual rotation around the sun. "The system proposed by Copernicus required such a reversal of all current scientific and religious thought as to man's place in the physical universe that violent opposition arose and even learned men were slow to accept its possibility."[4]

1851 A.D.

The actual daily rotation of the earth ultimately became demonstrated by the application of physical laws discovered concerning the movement of pendulums. "The first scientific proof of the rotation of the earth

---

[4]Charles P. Olivier, "Copernican System", Encyclopedia Americana, Vol. 7, 1957 ed. p. 649.

5

which admits of no argument is the device invented by Jean Leon Foucault. In 1851 he suspended a long pendulum from the interior of the dome of the pantheon in Paris."[5] It was simply a heavy iron ball attached to the end of a long thin cable. The length was adjusted so that the ball swung across a circular rail at the base of the huge dome. A ring of sand was made by distributing the sand around the top of the railing. The ball was drawn aside and the pendulum's movement was started, allowing the ball to swing across the rail. A thin wire attached to the under side of the ball made a mark in the sand on each side of the ring as it swung across. The direction of swing was changing showing the earth's rotation beneath the pendulum.

Foucault pointed out that in all the laws of nature there was no force acting directly upon his pendulum to make it change its direction of swing. Then the only answer there could be was that the earth must be turning beneath the pendulum. It is easy to imagine how the earth could turn beneath the swinging pendulum if the experiment below could be performed over the north or south pole. See Fig. 2.

3. THE EARTH IS NOT SUPPORTED

Bible Writers: 2000 B.C.
Job 26:7, "He . . . hangs the earth on nothing."

ANALYSIS: A clear statement in unscientific terms.

FACT: Job wrote that the earth is not mechanically supported.

---

[5]Alexander F. Morrison Planetarium, "Our Spinning Earth", California Academy of Sciences, 1965, p. 3.

PENDULUM ILLUSTRATION

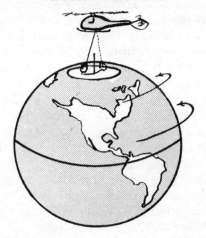

Fig. 2

EXAMPLE OF SIMILAR FORCES HOLDING BALL

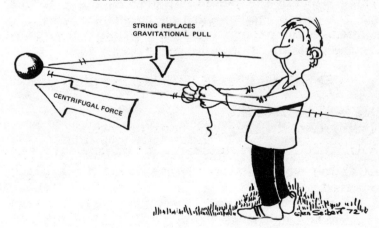

STRING REPLACES
GRAVITATIONAL PULL

CENTRIFUGAL FORCE

Fig. 3

History of Science: Pre-1543 A.D.
As previously noted, the world's scholars and scientists, with the exception of a few early Greeks, believed in the Ptolemy system that the earth was rigidly supported and all movement was in the heavens.

1687 A.D.
It was the invention of the telescope in 1608, by a Dutch optician, Hans Lippershey, that gave the scientists the ultimate tool that would unlock the secrets of our earth's position in space.

In succeeding years the development of the telescope led Sir Isaac Newton to discover that the earth's weight is not supported, but suspended in its orbit by attraction to the sun. Newton published this finding in his "Principia" in 1687. In it he presented for the first time what now is referred to as the "Law of Universal Gravitation". To understand the magnitude of the problem, the earth weighs six billion trillion (6×10^{21}) tons. To replace the gravitational pull of our sun, it would take the strength of a steel cable 8000 miles in diameter. See Fig. 3.

1839 A.D.
The parallactic orbit of stars was discovered. This is a shift in the apparent direction of a heavenly body caused by a change in the relative position of the observer which gives him a three-dimensional view, thus it was seen that the earth was not mechanically supported.

It was also noted that there were small annual displacements in the apparent position of many fixed stars. This was seen as proof of our earth's annual orbit around the sun.

1930 A.D.
Sir Isaac Newton was the first to demonstrate that a prism can split light into a color spectrum in the year 1666. This led to the later development of the spectroscope which became a practical scientific instrument in 1859. The modern telescope combined with the spectroscope in 1930 was used to further prove the daily rotation of the earth and its annual revolution about the sun.

"We now have several absolute proofs lacking before the days of telescope and spectroscopes." [6]

Today's scientists are revealing wonders of the vast universe to us through development of new and powerful tools. Bearing in mind that astronomers were given their first significant tool less than four centuries ago, let us now turn our attention from this planet to the discoveries of the surrounding heavens.

The writers of the Bible comprehended three heavens. The first was the atmosphere common to life and flying things; the second was the starry firmament; and the third was the place of God's throne. These ancient writers had much to say about this second heaven. Therefore we shall check their knowledge against the proven facts that man's recent inventions have revealed.

4. THE UNIVERSE IS A CONTINUOUSLY SPREADING EXPANSE

Bible Writers: 1491-1451 B.C.
Genesis 1:8, "And God called the expanse heaven." In verses 14-19 it is recorded that the sun and stars were "in the expanse of the heavens."

---

[6]Charles P. Olivier, "Copernican System", Ibid.

628-588 B.C.
Jeremiah 31:37, "Thus says the Lord, If the heavens above can be measured, . . . then I will also cast off all the offspring of Israel."

ANALYSIS: What did Moses mean by the word "expanse", or "firmament" as it is sometimes called? The Hebrew word is "raqiya" and derives its root meaning from the "spreading out" of something pounded, such as metal as it is continuously beaten with a metalsmith's hammer. Thus the word "firmament" is defined as a "spreading out expanse" which is a present continuous action and implies no limit has yet been reached. This word is used only in connection with the physical heavens, and never refers to the area of God's throne. By applying the literal meaning to the above passage we see Moses declaring — the "spreading out expanse" is called heaven, and the sun, moon, and stars are in the "spreading out expanse" of heaven.

FACT: Moses stated that the visible heaven, is made up of a continuously spreading expanse, while Jeremiah referred to the fact that men cannot complete the measurement of it.

History of Science: Pre-1800 A.D.
Until the aid of modern instruments provided man with the means of measuring the heavens, all mankind's theories and philosophical thoughts considered the universe as finite and limited. In many instances whole civilizations believed the heavenly bodies were close enough to permit gods to live on them and visually observe happenings on earth. The more observant men thought in terms of "hundreds of thousands of miles". Many wondered as did Job "Behold the height of the stars, how high are they?"

10

"In looking back to former ideas of the universe and comparing them with those current today, one is struck with the fact that the supposed size of the universe has increased almost incredibly, not only since the days of the Greek philosophers, but during the past generation." [7]

1835-1901 A.D.
The leading American astronomer of his time, Simon Newcomb, believed the most distant star only 3260 light-years away. A light-year is the distance over which light can travel in a year's time. It is approximately six trillion (6×10^{12}) miles. To grasp the concept of one light-year it can be related to the following. The earth is approximately 25,000 miles around the Equator and light will travel around it seven times in one second. The distance to the sun is about 3,700 times the distance around the earth, and therefore it takes sunlight 500 seconds to reach us. It would take 66,000 of these earth-to-sun units of distance to equal one light-year.

1917 A.D.
Albert Einstein in this year wrote his General Theory of Relativity in which he conceived the universe as finite, unbounded, and static, a premise that was disproved ten years later.

At Lick Observatory Heber D. Curtise first discovered spiral nebulae (nebulae are stellar or space bodies and gases). These appear to the naked eye to be only a star in our galaxie, but when Curtise turned a powerful telescope on one it proved to be composed of billions of suns comprising a flat spiral disk shape.

[7]Charles P. Oliver, "Universe", Encyclopedia Americana, Vol. 27, 1957 ed. p. 573.

1924 A.D.

Until 1924 it was not known whether these spiral nebulae were inside or outside our galaxy. Edwin P. Hubble using the Mount Wilson reflector proved these to be outside our galaxy and to be galaxies or island universes comparable to our own Milky Way.

In 1928 Edwin Hubble and M. Humason used the spectroscope in analyzing star light. Together they discovered the law connecting the red shift of a galaxy with its distance, now called Hubble's law.

1950 A.D.

In 1948, after twenty years of planning and construction, the 200-inch instrument at Mount Palomar reached out two billion light-years into space disclosing two important facts. First, there is a homogeneous distribution of nebula throughout space. It showed the universe consisted of many galaxies, probably trillions of them. Secondly, it revealed all these galaxies were moving away from us, the further off the nebula, the faster the velocity. This latter development is shown by a definite "red shift" in their spectra.

This velocity observation is accomplished by directing the light of a given nebula into a spectroscope which defracts the light into a color spectrum. The spectrum is composed of light separated according to its wave length, running from the longer wave lengths of red at one end to violet, the shorter waves, at the other. Each element when burned, produces light of certain definite wave lengths. These appear in the spectrum as a definite pattern of lines, always at the same place in the spectrum unless the source of light is relatively moving toward or away from the observer. If the source is receding, the pattern of lines for any element will appear farther toward the red than they would if the source were stationary with respect to the observer.

The shifting of the special lines is used extensively to determine the velocities of planets and stars with respect to the earth. Practically all spectra of galaxies have their lines shifted toward the red. These shifts are very great for the more distant galaxies and less for the closer ones. This shift has become commonly known as the "red shift". The concept of the expanding universe can be compared to the expanding volume within an inflating balloon. With this proof that the universe is expanding, the concept of a limited universe finally came to an end.

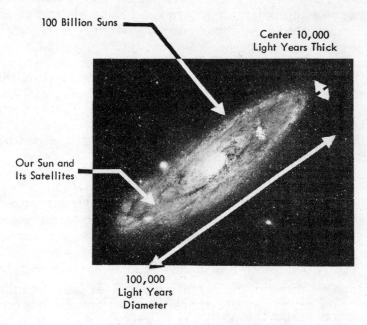

100 Billion Suns

Center 10,000
Light Years Thick

Our Sun and
Its Satellites

100,000
Light Years
Diameter

MILKY WAY GALAXY
Fig. 4

5. THE STARS ARE INNUMERABLE

Bible Writers: 628-588 B.C.
Jeremiah 33:22, "As the host of heaven cannot be counted, and the sand of the sea cannot be measured,. . ."

63 A.D.
Hebrews 11:12, ". . . As the stars of the heaven in number, and innumerable as the sand which is by the seashore."

FACT: Both writers contended that the number of stars are as innumerable as are the grains of sand of all the sea shores.

History of Science: 150 B.C.
Hipparchus taught that there were less than 3,000 stars.

150 A.D.
Ptolemy counted 1056 stars and claimed the actual number would not exceed 3,000.

1608 A.D.
Galileo used a telescope the first year it was invented and being the first to discover there are so many stars, he announced the number was innumerable.

1924 A.D.
Gradually, through the invention of better instruments, the number grew till there is now numbered one hundred billion suns in our galaxy and there is estimated to be trillions of galaxies of which ours is average. To comprehend the possibility of counting

stars, if a man were to count the suns just in our Milky Way Galaxy at the rate of 200 per minute, it would take him 1,000 years.

Pause one moment in this study, and attempt to comprehend this God of the universe that Christians worship. Are not his intelligence and power, as manifested by the stars, beyond comprehension?

"Lift up your eyes on high
And see who has created these stars,
The One who leads forth their host by number
He calls them all by name;
Because of the greatness of His might and the
    strength of His power
Not one of them is missing."   Isaiah 40:26

"He counts the number of stars;
He gives names to all of them"   Psalm 147:4

This is the Divine Being that calls Christians his "adopted children" and asks them to speak to him in prayer. As for those who choose not to believe in God, the apostle Paul warned, "For since the creation of the world His invisible attributes, His eternal power and divine nature, have been clearly seen, being understood through what has been made, so that they are without excuse."   Romans 1:20

6. STARS EMIT SOUND

Bible Writers: 2000 B.C.
Job 38:7, ". . . the morning stars sang together."

ANALYSIS: The Hebrew word for "sang" is "ranan" and pertains to the emittance of a loud creak, shrill, or stredulous sound.

FACT: Job declared stars emit loud, shrill, stredulous sounds that are audible.

15

History of Science : 1940 A.D.
In an attempt to determine whether stars emit sound, Grote Raber tried to detect radio waves from the sun. His results were negative.

1942 A.D.
Raber tried again with "inconclusive" results. The same year United States Army scientists were testing secret radar equipment developed for detecting German aircraft. This equipment used a wave length of 400 to 500 centimeters. Suddenly in February of 1942, the radar sets received extremely high noise so loud they could not be operated. At first it was thought to be a form of German "jamming". The direction of the sound was soon traced however, and found to be caused by the activities of a sun spot.

This discovery gave birth to the radio telescope as a research tool after the war. It is now known that radio waves that enter our atmosphere vary in length from 0.8 centimeters to 17 meters. The natural ear is not designed to hear the shrill of the stars.

Nov. 1, 1963 A.D.
The science of Astrophysics is concerned with the mechanics of all nebulae in the universe. Its newest tool was set in operation at Arecilo, Puerto Rico. This is the world's largest and most powerful radio telescope. Its 1000 foot diameter reflector is set within a natural depression in the earth and with this instrument astronomers have discovered objects in the heavens unlike anything previously observed before.

These are so odd that they cannot be explained as yet. They are starlike in appearance, but of tremendous size, are strong radio sources, and if indications are correct, they shine with the equivalent intensity of a trillion suns. Known as Quasars, they are moving away at great speeds and must be near the edge of the known universe. An announcement from Mount Wilson Observatory placed one Quasar as the most distant object known. The computed red shift of this Quasar indicates a recession of 149,000 miles per second.

The strangest feature of Radio Astronomy is that the most powerful radio sources cannot be identified optically with anything at all, indicating radio telescopes might be seeing much farther into space than optical ones.[8]

7. HEAVENS CONTROLLED BY ORDINANCES

Bible Writers: 2000 B.C.
Job 38:33, "Do you know the ordinances of the heavens, or fix their rule over the earth?"

1015 B.C.
David wrote of the heavens in Psalms 19:4, "Their line is gone out through all the earth."

1033-975 B.C.
Solomon stated in Proverbs 8:28, "He made firm the skies above."

628-588 B.C.
Jeremiah 31:35, "Thus says the Lord, Who gives . . . the fixed order of the moon and stars for light by night,"

ANALYSIS: The word "line" in Psalms 19 is a Hebrew word which refers to literally having "rule" or "measured control", such as a city's boundary line.

8William Bonnor, The Mystery of the Expanding Universe, (The Macmillan Co., N.Y., 1964) p. 68.

FACT: These four writers collectively wrote that all heavenly bodies are governed by ordinances. They held that these ordinances were:

a. Being "firm" or "hard", unchangeable
b. Being consistent and harmonious with one another because they are governed by one intelligent source
c. The heavens physically have a measured control, or "rule" over this planet.

History of Science: 700 B.C.

The technical elements of astrology came from Babylon and Egypt. The first known horoscopes are recorded in cuneiform tablets dated 410 B.C. from Egypt, although the technical elements of the twelve houses of the Zodiac came from Babylon.[9]

1687 A.D.

Until this year it was assumed the stars' movements could control and foretell men's acts upon the earth. This pseudo science of Astrology is based on the assumption that the movement of the stars are irregular and not governed by "firm ordinances".

Sir Isaac Newton, in this year, led the world to acknowledge that all heavenly bodies, including this planet, are regulated by what he called "Celestial Mechanics". This discovery of the "Law of Universal Gravitation" was made possible by the development of the telescope, as previously noted. Such men as Claudius Ptolemy not only were astronomers, but indulged in Astrology, usually for profit. True science was hindered by such practice and superstition. Ptolemy was typical in that "his scientific investigations

---

9George Sarton, A History Of Science, (Harvard U. Press, 1959) p. 164 & 316.

in the field of natural astrology were marred by his indulgence in the casting of horoscopes".[10]

Astrology lasted in Europe until the middle of the 17th century before declining. It still flourishes however in Asia and Africa and is a means of livelihood to many charlatans who prey upon the ignorant people in all countries.

1974 A.D.

Note the phenomenal increase of horoscopes in this country. This ancient form of idolatry is found in over 1700 daily newspapers, numerous magazines and daily radio broadcasts. God had an answer for this "star worship" 3500 years ago, "You shall not make for yourself an idol, or any likeness of what is in heaven above,"   Exodus 20:4.

Today's scientist realizes that the movement of the stars is the most precise clockwork known.

8. THERE ARE MANY SUNS

Bible Writers: 1491-1451 B.C.
Moses spoke of the stars in heaven in the following passage, Genesis 1:16, 17, "And God made the two great lights; the greater light to govern the day, and the lesser light to govern the night; He made the stars also. And God placed them in the expanses of the heavens to give light on the earth."

ANALYSIS: The word "light", in referring to heavenly light sources, is the Hebrew word "Maor", which literally means "light container or luminous body". This

---

[10]Fergus J. Wood, "Ptolemy", Encyclopedia Americana, Vol. 22, 1957 ed. p. 753.

is an accurate description of stars being their own source of light. Both stars and our sun are called "luminous bodies" thus recognizing their sameness.

The words in verse 16 "He made" and "also" are not found in the original text, but were supplied by the imagination of the translators. The verse therefore should read, "and the lesser to rule the night, the stars."

The Hebrew definition for "asah", the word "made" in the first part of verse 16, is "constituted and appointed". This is the same use as when in Israel certain cities were appointed to be "cities of refuge"[1]. Thus we note the day that God appointed the stars and sun to their purpose of giving light to the earth.

FACT: Moses had knowledge that all stars are suns as our sun, and each contains its own source of light. He further prohibited their use in worship to God.

History of Science: Pre-1650 A.D.
All civilizations, until the 17th century, placed a certain amount of religious significance in the heavenly bodies. Some thought them to be gods or deities while others considered them to only reflect the light of our sun. None are known to believe stars equivalent to our sun.

1859 A.D.
The newly developed spectro-telescope was used to analyze star light. Only then was it proved that stars are their own source of light and equivalent to our sun.

---

[1]Psalms 138:8,9.

II
Geology

9. FOUNDATION OF THE EARTH

Bible Writers: 2000 B.C.
Job speaks of the "foundations of the earth" in Job 38:4, 6.
"On what were its bases sunk?"
He adds that the shore lines were fixed at the same time, Job 38:8-11.
"Or who enclosed the sea with doors, . . . when
I placed boundaries on it,
And I set a bolt and doors,
And I said, 'Thus far you shall come, but no further;
And here shall your proud waves stop'?"

1033-975 B.C.
David wrote in Psalms 104:5,
"He established the earth upon its foundations,
So that it will not totter forever and ever."
Solomon spoke in Proverbs 8:29,
"He set for the sea its boundary,
So that the water should not transgress His
command,
When He marked out the foundations of the earth."

628-588 B.C.
Jeremiah 31:37, Portrays the impossibility for man to accomplish the following, "the foundations of the earth searched out below . . ."

21

ANALYSIS: As we have already observed, Job wrote that the earth is "hung upon nothing" while it rotates. Solomon recorded that the earth is "spherical". Yet both men, as well as many other Bible writers, speak of the earth as having "foundations".

Job declared that these "foundations" of the earth (dry land as described in Genesis 1:10) to be designed and measured when laid. In the 6th verse a different Hebrew word is used to describe these "foundations". The word translated "bases" is from "eden", which literally means "foundation sockets". Therefore this verse would literally read, concerning dry land, "On what were its foundation sockets made to sink into?"

Job writes that this design "shut up the sea with doors", and "mark out for it" its permanent "bounds".

Jeremiah implies that man will not be able to "search out" the earth's foundation "below". He parallels this with the impossibility of man to measure the heavens or cause the laws of the universe to depart from God.

FACT: These Bible writers wrote of an unmovable foundation that lay "below" their feet. One that "marked out" for the sea its permanent "boundary". A "foundation" that cannot be "searched out", one that supported dry land by providing sockets for its "bases" to lay in.

History of Science: Pre-1934 A.D.

What supports the ground beneath our feet has always been a subject of interest to mankind. Men have speculated many varied foundations, including animals, pillars, etc. The theory that had world-wide acceptance in the first third of the 20th century, concluded that the earth has NO foundation, but was full of hot molten nickel-steel and covered with a floating thin crust. This theory was based on the fact that the earth increases in temperature as it is penetrated at the rate of 1°C per 100 feet, and the observation of the earth's crust moving about during an earthquake, as though it were on a fluid base. The heavy liquid core was thought to occasionally erupt through volcanoes, and the flow indicated that the core temperature would be about 2000°C. Knowing the rate of heat increase through the crust, coupled with the temperature assumption of the molten core beneath, the crust was estimated to have an average depth of 20 miles.

1935 A.D.

The development of precision chronometers, seismographs, and recording instruments brought about a revolution in men's knowledge of the structure of this planet. When accurate measurements of time and earth vibration became possible, scientists discovered that an earth tremor caused two types of shock waves to appear. One was a transverse wave, like the ripples in a bowl of jello when it is shaken. This is called an "S" wave, for "shake" wave. The other is known as a "P" wave for "push" wave, and is a compression wave. The transmission characteristics are such that "S" waves disappear and will not be transmitted through three-dimensionally contained fluids, while "P" waves will travel through either fluids or solids, although the rate through will be slower.

1960 A.D.

In recording earth tremors of large magnitude with these precision tools, it has been noted that if the quake was on the other side of the planet from the seismograph recording station, only a "P" wave would appear at several intervals, each with varying magnitudes. Yet, a quake in the near vicinity of a seismograph station would register both a strong "P" and "S" wave. From the compiling of earth tremor data, the scientists have concluded that the earth has a liquid core, but only 2100 miles in radius, with a dense Mantle Rock 1800 miles thick over it.

1964 A.D.

By using sensitive seismic instruments that transmit information about the earth's interior, geologists learned much during the 1964 Alaskan earthquake. Geologists have cooperated in a major study of this earthquake using information from 100 stations located in more than 50 countries. Measurements of seismic wave velocities indicated that the upper surface of the mantle rock changes from about five miles below sea level at the edges of the continents down to depths averaging 310 miles. Thus, a bowl is formed for the continental material extending deep into the foundation Mantle Rock.[12]

With today's chronometers we can tell the speed with which these waves travel through the earth, thus establishing the densities of the materials. The Mantle Rock provides a constant velocity path for "P" shocks of 8.1 km/sec., indicating very heavy granite type rock. This Mantle Rock is now known to be the "foundation" of our planet. Its inside contains a fluid core and its outside shapes the continents and sea basins. It is covered by only two to three miles of sediment under the oceans, then it dips deep beneath the continents providing sockets for the six continents to rest in. Thus, scientists have learned that the Mantle Rock gives this

[12]William M. Merrill, "Geology", Americana Annual, 1965 ed. p. 294.

terrestial sphere the division of earth and water on its surface by providing a fundamentally different geological structure for both. See Fig. 5.

EARTH CROSS SECTION

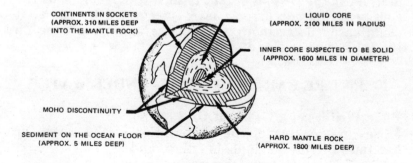

CONTINENTS IN SOCKETS
(APPROX. 310 MILES DEEP
INTO THE MANTLE ROCK)

LIQUID CORE
(APPROX. 2100 MILES IN RADIUS)

INNER CORE SUSPECTED TO BE SOLID
(APPROX. 1600 MILES IN DIAMETER)

MOHO DISCONTINUITY

SEDIMENT ON THE OCEAN FLOOR
(APPROX. 5 MILES DEEP)

HARD MANTLE ROCK
(APPROX. 1800 MILES DEEP)

Fig. 5

1973 A.D.

The Deep Sea Drilling Project, funded by the National Science Foundation, and managed by Scripps Institute of Oceanography, used the unique vessel, Glomar Challenger, which incorporates the latest advances in offshore drilling technology. After drilling 246 holes in 154 sites in the ocean floor, the conclusion was reached that the ocean floor is of different geological origin than the continents and that it has never been dry land. It was found that subterranean heat and upheaval causes the ocean floor to grow and slowly slide toward the continents.[13] This new drilling platform has provided information that the continents have always been independent of the ocean floor, and that the shore lines are relatively fixed.

The theory that movement of the ocean floor has caused continents to drift is impractical on many points, including the impossibility of a thin sheet of sliding ocean floor on top of the Mantle Rock to move a massive continent anchored in a 310 mile deep socket in the Mantle. It can be noted that if such a movement of the continents has occurred, as is speculated by some, it could easily be accounted for in the arranging done on the third day by God.[14]

10. ENTIRE EARTH HAS BEEN UNDER WATER

Bible Writers: 1491-1451 B.C.

Moses in speaking of the preparation of the earth for habitation wrote in Genesis 1:2, 6, and 9,

"And the earth was formless and void."

---

[13]University of California, San Diego, Scripps Institution of Oceanography Deep Sea Drilling Project, "Release Number 164", 1971, p. 1.
[14]Genesis 1:9,10.

"Then God said, Let there be an expanse in the midst
of the waters, and let it separate the waters from
the waters."

"Then God said, 'Let the waters below the heavens
be gathered into one place, and let the dry land
appear'; and it was so."

Again Moses spoke of the earth later being covered
completely with water during the life of Noah, Genesis
7:19, 20, 24.

"And the water prevailed more and more upon the
earth; so that all the high mountains everywhere under
the heavens were covered. The water prevailed fifteen
cubits higher, and the mountains were covered. . . .
And the water prevailed upon the earth one hundred
and fifty days."

1033-975 B.C.

David also spoke of the time the waters were separated
in Psalms 104:6-9.

"Thou didst cover it with the deep as with a garment;
The waters were standing above the mountains.
At Thy rebuke they fled;
At the sound of Thy thunder they hurried away.
The mountains rose; the valleys sank down
To the place which Thou didst establish for them.
Thou didst set a boundary that they may not pass
over;
That they may not return to cover the earth."

ANALYSIS: Moses wrote of a time when the earth was
"formless" and "void", meaning "without purpose". A
time when water covered everything. It was at this
time the waters were separated and gathered to form
the seas and the moisture in the atmosphere.

He wrote that during the Flood the earth was

covered a second time. This was after animal life was in existence and accounts for the sealife found on all mountain ranges.

FACT: In summarizing these writings, we see they were aware that this planet was twice engulfed with water. Both times covering the tallest mountains.

History of Science: Pre-1669 A.D.
"Before Geology could assume the character of a separate scientific discipline, the basic sciences, the knowledge of animals and plants, and the geography of continents and oceans had to advance sufficiently to provide a focus for thought concerning minerals, rocks, fossils, and landscapes. But above all, intelligent observation of what is seen in nature had to be substituted for the scholastic habit of reasoning in terms of abstract concepts."[15]

1669 A.D.
Geology as a science was initiated in Italy when the Danish anatomist, Nicolas Steno, turned his attention to the structure of Tuscany, his adopted country. His study of animal anatomy led him into observations of mountain rock formations in which the fossils were found. The small book he published concerning his findings marked the beginning of systematic geological investigations.

1885 A.D.
Edward Suess was one of the first geologists to publish a study based on the geologic framework of all countries. His research led to his discovery that all land

[15]Walter H. Bucher, "Geology", Encyclopedia Americana, Vol. 12, 1957 ed. p. 455a.

surface has been under water, especially in his observations of the world's mountain ranges. It is now evident that even the oldest rock formations show traces of sedimentary origin.

11. ALL SEAS LIE IN ONE BED

Bible Writers: 1491-1451 B.C.
Moses wrote of the formation of the Seas in Genesis 1:9, 10.

"Then God said, 'Let the waters below the heavens be gathered into one place, and let the dry land appear'; and it was so. And God called the dry land earth, and the gathering of the waters He called seas."

FACT: Moses recorded that all waters stood in "one place", or "bed" as we now call it. He said that waters name was Seas (plural), thus revealing he understood there was more than one body of water in this common bed.

History of Science: 1520 A.D.
As we already noted, it was not until the introduction of the compass and improved sailing vessels that the voyages of Columbus, Magellan, and others were made possible. "Ferdinand Magellan was probably the first explorer to attempt Oceanographical research on the great voyage which established the fact that a ship could sail around the earth."[16] These men's discoveries led to establishing the fact that all large bodies of water are inter-joined.

[16] John Scott Douglas, Story of the Ocean, (N.Y., Dodd, Mead & Co., 1952), p. 4.

1960 A.D.

As noted previously, the foundation underlying the seas is of such structure that it is now considered by scientists to have always been a common sea bed and never dry land. Recent oil and oceanographic coring have offered further proof by revealing only fossilized sea life in the ocean floor sediment.

Further evidence that the ocean floors have never been dry land is provided by off-shore drilling. The core samples brought up reveal only sedimentary deposits containing sea life.

III
Oceanography

12. RECESSES OF THE DEEP

Bible Writers: 2000 B.C.
Job 38:16, "Have you walked in the recesses of the deep?"

1015 B.C.
David in a psalm spoke of these recesses, 2 Samuel 22:16,
"The channels of the sea appeared,
The foundations of the world were laid bare."

ANALYSIS: "Channels" can literally mean "canyon" or "crevasse". This psalm of David was written using the form of Hebrew poetry where the second verse usually repeated the thought of the first, but in different words. He compared the exposing of "the channels of the sea" to the laying bare "the foundations of the world".

FACT: Job and David spoke of "recesses" or "channels" of the sea. David claimed the bottom of these would penetrate to "the foundations of the world".

History of Science: 1504 A.D.
Juan de la Costa made the first sounding in this year. They were made in shallow water near the coast, and placed on his map. This effort did nothing to change the universal opinion that the ocean floors were flat, sandy beds like our deserts.

1840 A.D.
"In 1840 Sir James Clark Rose made the first true oceanic sounding, reaching a depth of nearly 2000 fathoms with a weight on the end of a hemp line."[17]

1873 A.D.
The British ship "Challenger" was the first vessel outfitted solely for sea exploration. The now famous Challenger Expedition (1872-76) marks the beginning of modern deep-sea exploration. This expedition found one isolated depth of 4,500 fathoms (5½ miles) in the Pacific Ocean, thus being the first to discover an underwater trench or canyon.

1911 A.D.
Echo-sounding was introduced by Reginald A. Fessenden although it remained undeveloped until World War II. This method of measuring the depth of a body of water utilizes radio signals or explosive charges by placing them just beneath the surface and directing their discharge in the direction of the ocean floor. These radio waves or shock waves then travel to the floor and bounce or reflect back to a receiver. The time intervals between the sending and receipt of a signal can be translated into distance.

1945 A.D.
"Before the invention of echo-sounding equipment it was generally thought that the bottom of the oceans would present the appearance of plains, plateaus, and gently rolling terrain. Now we know that it has valleys

[17]Francis P. Shepard, The Earth Beneath the Ocean, (John Hopkins) p. 161.

and mountain ranges, and even canyons, to equal all the forms we find on land."[18]

Echo-sounding research used in submarine warfare later developed into a practical scientific tool. After the war the U.S. Navy equipped their vessels with echo-sounding and recording equipment. Since soundings can be taken while the ship is moving, much of the ocean floor began to be mapped.

The systematic crisscrossing of both private and military boats using sounding equipment has, since 1945, given us our current knowledge. We now know these gigantic under water canyons circle the globe at great depths, the deepest recorded to date being the Marianas Trench near the Philippines which is over seven miles deep, the Tonga Trench which is a mile deeper than Mt. Everest is high, and Peru-Chile Trench has one wall that rises over 42,000 feet. Our Grand Canyon is but a miniature of the sea canyons.

1964 A.D.

The first humans to travel along the bottom of an ocean trench did it in the 200-ton French bathyscaph "Archimede". Ten trips 27,500 feet deep were made to the bottom of the Puerto Rico Trench, the deepest known part of the Atlantic Ocean. These trips were part of Operation Deepscan, a joint Franco-American oceanographic project. The most surprising discovery made by the Archimede was that the trench is terraced into steps hundreds of miles long and about ten feet high on both its north and south walls. Other discoveries included the great amount of sea life that

---

[18]Maurice Ewing and Bruce C. Heezen, "Deep Sea Exploration", Encyclopedia Americana Vol. 8, 1957 ed. p. 580.

exists at the bottom where pressures reach 12,000 pounds per square inch.

1970 A.D.

The "Glomar Challenger" is being used as a drilling platform as previously described in the section "Foundation Of The Earth". Since 1970 the drilling for core samples has taken place in the trenches through a water depth of 20,000 feet, with a penetration into the ocean floor of 3,334 feet.[19] A new drill hole re-entry technique will allow even deeper penetration in the future.

The Deep Sea Drilling Project has provided an explanation for the formation of the trenches. The spreading ocean floor continually moves from the Mid-ocean ridge toward the continental crust, where it slides down against the continental "socket foundation" and is absorbed in the Mantle. Thus, a deep trench is formed at the edge of the continental shelf.[20] See Fig. 6.

How true it is, as written by David, when "the channels of the sea appear, the foundations of the world are laid bare."

1971 A.D.

For the first time in Man's history a complete map of the ocean floor has been compiled and was made available, showing the complete "recesses of the deep".

---

[19]M. N. A. Peterson, Deep Sea Drilling Project Reasons And Results, (Deep Sea Drilling Project, 1970) p. 1.
[20]Deep Sea Drilling Project, (National Science Foundation, 1970) p. 12.

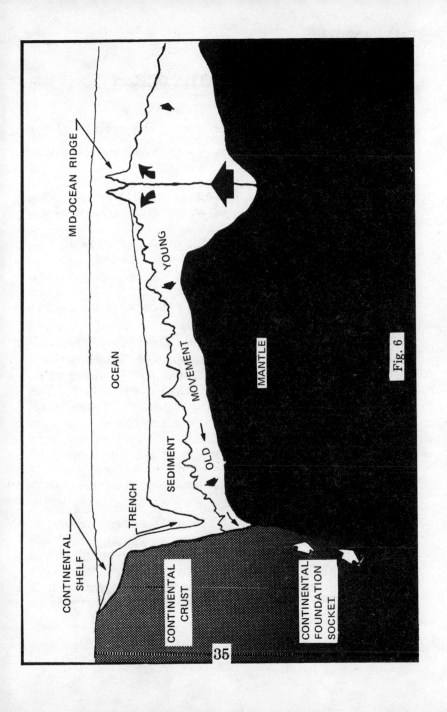

CONTINENTAL SHELF

MID-OCEAN RIDGE

OCEAN

TRENCH

SEDIMENT

YOUNG

MOVEMENT

OLD

MANTLE

Fig. 6

CONTINENTAL CRUST

CONTINENTAL FOUNDATION SOCKET

35

13. SPRINGS IN THE OCEAN

Bible Writers: 2000 B.C.
Job 38:16a, "Have you entered into the springs of the sea?"

1491-1451 B.C.
Moses, in his account of the flood in Noah's time, recorded what one source of water was: Genesis 7:11, and 8:2,
"All the fountains of the great deep burst open."
"The fountains of the deep . . . were closed."

1033-975 B.C.
Solomon wrote in Proverbs 8:28, concerning the earth's origin,
"When the springs of the deep became fixed."

FACT: The composite information of these writers shows that they understood there to be underwater "springs" or "fountains" on the ocean floor. The openings were large enough for a person to walk into. They have been a source of water since the oceans were formed, including an exceptionally heavy flow for forty days during which time water rose to cover the mountains.

History of Science: 1930 A.D.
Unknown sources were found to be providing fresh water welling up to the surface in the ocean. Some of these sources have been discovered, by using deep sea diving equipment, to be large underground rivers flowing within the continental shelf. Their headwaters are at a high inland mountainous elevation while their outlet is where the continental shelf drops abruptly to the ocean floor.

1945 A.D.

It was not until Oceanography research ships plied the seas after World War II, using the latest equipment including explosive charges for their depth recorders, that underwater volcanoes were discovered. There are estimated to be at least 10,000 volcanoes dotting the floor of the Pacific Ocean alone. Many stand tall and narrow extending thousands of feet high. Their underwater appearance would be as a forest land of chimneys protruding from the ocean floor to various heights.

Research by Dr. William W. Rubey of the U.S. Geological Survey has shown that the present rate of water release from underwater volcanoes, fumaroles (secondary volcanic outlets), and hot springs releases 430 million tons per year.[21] The earth's heat drives the entrapped water from underground molten rock and forces it out through one of these natural openings.

Dr. Lawrence J. Kulp of Columbia University has shown this release of new water is possible since the earth is estimated to have ½ of 1% of its weight in water entrapped within its rocks. Dr. Kulp's measurements resulted in the following conclusions,[22]

a. Measured water in a rock averages ½ to 1% of its weight.

b. The earth weighs about 6 billion trillion (6×10^{21}) tons.

c. Therefore ½% of the earth's weight is 30 million trillion (30×10^{19}) tons.

d. If 6% escaped from the interior of the earth, it would be enough to fill all the seas, or 2 million trillion (2×10^{18}) tons.

[21]William J. Cromie, Exploring the Secrets of the Sea, (H. J. Prentice-Hall, Inc., 1962) p. 15.
[22]Same as above note. Ibid.

14. OCEAN CURRENTS

Bible Writers: 1015 B.C.
David said in Psalms 8:8 God has subjected all things to men, including:
"Whatever passeth through the paths of the sea."
ANALYSIS: The Hebrew word "paths" carries the literal meaning of "customary roads".
FACT: David knew there were "paths" or "customary roads" in the sea, and that sea life "passed through" these paths.

History of Science: 1855 A.D.
Matthew Fontaine Maury is called "The Pathfinder of the Seas". This American is the father of today's oceanography and responsible for the establishment of Annapolis Academy. A statue of Maury stands in Richland, Virginia; charts of the sea in one hand, Bible in the other. Until Maury's efforts there were no charts or sailing lanes. One day during a temporary illness, his eldest son was reading to him from the Bible, and read Psalms 8:8. Maury stopped him and said, "read that again". After hearing it again, he exclaimed, "It is enough, if the word of God says there are paths in the sea, they must be there, and I am going to find them." Within a few years he had charted sea lanes and currents. His "Physical Geography of the Sea" was the first textbook of modern oceanography.

Since his discovery of the "paths of the sea" commercial fishermen have learned that schools of fish are frequently found passing through them in search of food that these currents carry along.

IV
Meteorology

15. WATER-VAPOR CYCLE

Bible Writers: 2000 B.C.
Job 36:27,28, "For He draws up the drops of water, they distil rain from the mist, which the clouds pour down, they drip on man abundantly."

1033-975 B.C.
Solomon wrote in his book Ecclesiastes 1:7,
"All the rivers flow into the sea, yet the sea is not full. To the place where the rivers flow, there they flow again."

ANALYSIS: The Hebrew and English definition of "distil" is to have the small moisture droplets of steam or vapor condense and collect into water drops large enough to become heavy and fall.

FACT: These Biblical writers recognized the basic mechanics of the water-vapor cycle. All rivers empty into the sea from higher ground. Drops of water are drawn up forming vapor clouds. These "mist" droplets are transported as clouds until they distill "in rain" and thus "return" the rivers to the place they start.

History of Science: 350 B.C.
Aristotle is accredited with being the first to comprehend the water-vapor cycle that produces rain. His "Meteorlogica" became standard treatise for 2000 years. In it he theorized clouds and rain are caused by

condensation of water-vapor from the atmosphere that had gotten there by evaporation of water at the surface of the earth. His observations concluded that this was only a localized cycle, where rain replaced the water in the area from which it had vaporized.

1520 A.D.
Until it was known that the earth was spherical, the common belief was that the rivers flowing into the oceans did not cause the ocean to rise because an equal amount of water was spilling off the ends of the earth. Before Magellan's discovery no scientist conceived the idea that it was the water of the ocean that was being cycled to provide the fresh water of the rivers.

1770 A.D.
It was not observed until the 18th century that clouds can transport moisture away from the area in which they were formed. From observations at only a few points, Benjamin Franklin was the first to recognize that individual storms move from place to place over the earth's surface. The river-to-sea-to-river water cycle was published by Benjamin Franklin from his observations, thus greatly aiding the study of weather by men. See Fig. 7.

1841 A.D.
Galileo invented the thermometer in 1593 A.D. and Evangelista Torricelli the barometer in 1643. With the aid of these instruments, "Espy was among the first to point out the importance of expansion and cooling of rising air in production of clouds".[23] Thus, the origin of the clouds was proved for the first time. It is now

[23]Joy S. Winston, "Meteorology", Encyclopedia Americana, Vol. 18, 1957 ed. p. 714.

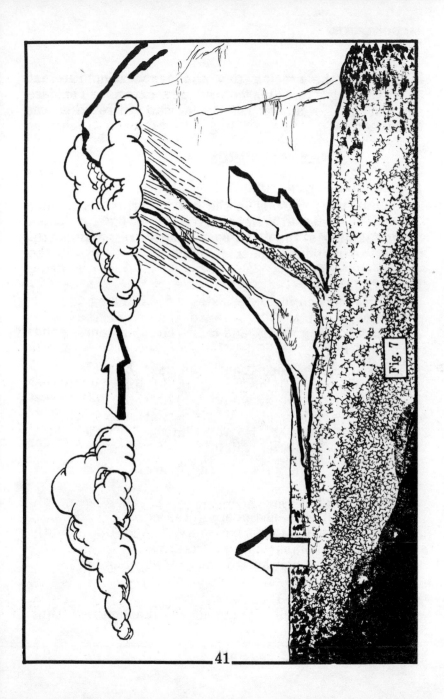

Fig. 7

known that the precipitation and evaporation rate is approximately 16,000,000 tons per second. This is equivalent to an annual rainfall for the entire earth of three feet.

16. AIR CIRCULATION

Bible Writers: 2000 B.C.
Job wrote the following in the book bearing his name: "When He imparted weight to the wind" (28:25); "Out of the chamber of the south comes the storm, and out of the scattering winds the cold" (37:9).

1033-975 B.C.
Solomon recorded in Ecclesiastes 1:6, "Blowing toward the south, then turning toward the north the wind continues turning along; and on its circular courses the wind returns."

ANALYSIS: The word "south" as used by Job is the same as Solomon's. It means "toward the south", hence a north wind. The verse would read literally, "out of the chamber of 'south heading winds' cometh the storm."

The word "weight" is from "mishgal" which is a "numerically calculated weight".

FACT: These men wrote of the following facts about the wind:
a. It had weight.
b. It came out of a "chamber" in the north.
c. The wind has a "circular courses" and flows south out of the chamber only to "return".
d. Storms travel southward out of this "chamber".

History of Science: 1643 A.D.
Evangelista Toricelli invented the barometer, thus

establishing as fact that air (wind) has weight, and measures 14.7 pounds per square inch at sea level.

1820 A.D.
About this year a German physicist and astronomer, Heinrich Brandes, collected observations and composed the first synoptic weather map.

1940 A.D.
As high flying jet aircraft and special observation balloons provided observations in the upper atmosphere, it was discovered that there is a basic pattern for air circulation. This is caused as the sun warms the ground, the ground heats the air. The sun rays strike obliquely at the poles causing the ground there to heat air less than at the equator. Warm air rises at the equator causing greater pressure at altitude. Air pressure at the ground level is greater at the poles because it is colder and denser. This pressure differential forces the air rising at the equator to flow north at high altitude until it cools and drops down at the pole, at which time it flows southward to fill the space at the equator being emptied by the rising air there. See Fig. 8.

The U.S. Weather Bureau recognized the importance of air masses as they accumulate at the North Pole, in effecting this hemisphere's storms. They have set up a weather station in the frozen land to help in weather prediction.

17. CLOUDS HAVE BALANCINGS

Bible Writers: 2000 B.C.
The following statements are found in Job's writing:
    37:16, "Do you know the balancings of the clouds?"

43

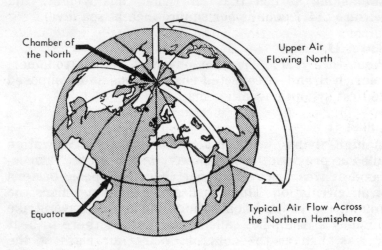

Fig. 8

38:37, "Who can number the clouds by wisdom?"
36:29, "Can any understand the spreadings of the clouds?"

FACT: It is written that clouds had "balancings", that there was something to be understood in the "spreading"; and that it took wisdom to know the right "number" of clouds that are necessary.

History of Science: 1860 B.C.
The Dutch meteorologist, Christoph Buys Ballot, formulated his famous law (Buys Ballot's Law) on the relation between pressure and wind. This was the start of our understanding of the balances that cause clouds.

1930 A.D.
Through the use of high altitude airplanes and weather balloons we continued to accumulate information concerning the cloud balancings of atmospheric pressures and temperatures.

1950 A.D.
High-altitude airplanes instrumented to detect electrical fields noted a high electrical energy flow upward from the top of a thunderstorm to the ionosphere (upper atmosphere). This showed a thundercloud can be considered as a negative electrical pump conveying a negative charge to the earth and a positive charge to the upper atmosphere. It was learned that the ionosphere continually discharged a current of 1800 Amperes to the earth over the whole globe. Instrumented warheads on research missiles revealed the total charge of the ionosphere would discharge completely in five minutes. Thunderstorms supply the reverse current necessary to maintain potential between the earth and upper atmosphere. It was estimated to take 1800 thunderstorms at any one instant to do this. Thus for the first time, man was able through acquired knowledge to guess the number of the clouds on our earth.

1960 A.D.
The Tiros Weather Satellite series has been of tremendous importance to atmospheric research. It has provided our first comprehensive view of the earth's cloud cover and showed large storm cloud formations to be spread spiral in nature. It proved the constance of the number of thunderstorms (1800) at any one time. The satellite is providing new data on the earth's heat

balance. "The general circulation of the atmosphere is regulated by heating of the earth by sunlight and cooling by reradiation to space. In order to better understand these processes, and in particular to obtain knowledge concerning the heat balance of the earth, detailed information concerning cloud cover is essential."[24]

Now we can daily watch "the spreading of the clouds" on the television weather analysis by those who "know the balancings of the clouds".

18. LIGHTNING CAUSES RAIN

Bible Writers: 2000 B.C.
Job wrote in Job 38:25-27, "Who has cleft a channel for the flood, or a way for the thunderbolt; to bring rain on a land without people, on a desert without a man in it, to satisfy the waste and desolate land, and to make seeds of grass to sprout?"

FACT: Job stated factually that lightning causes rain to fall and water ground where man does not live. He also speaks of a "way" that is "cleft" for the thunderbolt.

History of Science: 1930 A.D.
Using a high speed camera invented by Sir Charles Boys, Professor Basil Schonland in South Africa and Dr. Karl McEachron in the United States discovered that lightning developed only after "leaders", sometimes called "J-streamers", passed from the clouds down to the earth. These then made a path for the lightning stroke to discharge from the earth to the clouds. Only by slowing down the film, that had taken pictures at 100 miles per hour, could this initial probing weak

[24]David M. Gates, "Astronomy", The Americana Annual, 1961, p. 60.

electrical stroke be seen as it sought out a source of stored electrical energy in the earth, that it might provide a path for that energy to travel to the clouds. These "leaders" cleave a "way" for the thunderbolt.[25]

1960 A.D.
Meteorologists began for the first time to understand about the cause-and-effect of electrical charges on cloud formation and rain discharges. Facts were accumulating that indicated atmosphere electrical charges occur just before formation and dissipation of fog. A cloud droplet will not form until it has a small particle to form a water shell around. This cloud droplet is a long way from being a rain drop, for it takes about a million of them to make one drop. A research program was begun to determine if electrical activity had a part to play in the formation of a rain drop from the droplets of a cloud. If true, this would help explain why clouds laden with moisture could exist for days without losing any through rain.

1964 A.D.
The discovery was made that there are electrical phenomena of considerable magnitude accompanying tornadoes and the energy appears to be adequate to maintain the force of the tornado vortex.

One of the most promising studies was of rain gushes at the Grand Bahama Island by means of Cenimetric Radar. It showed the large drops of water responsible for a gush were not present before lightning occurrence, but were formed after discharge had taken place. Large drops were seen to collect in an extensive vertical

---

[25]J. H. Hagenguth, "Lightning", Encyclopedia Americana, Vol. 17, 1957 ed. p. 396b.

section of the cloud lying below the 0°C. level and in some tens of seconds could be followed in the subsequent fall toward the ground. The probable cause of this phenomenon is J-streamers, which are the multiple discharge streamers into the cloud of ground-to-ground lightning. The electrical discharge leaves the droplets which were in the discharge path with a charge opposite in polarity to the original, part of which still resides on droplets adjacent to streamer path. Neighboring drops are attracted to each other and form large drops which are heavy enough to overcome the cloud updraft and fall to earth.[26]

1965 A.D.

In this year the following demonstration proved to meteorologists that it takes electricity to cause rain. "An experiment in the laboratory demonstrates the theory that in the presence of an electrical field water droplets will combine to form raindrops. Tiny droplets like those in a cloud shot from a hypodermic needle will simply ricochet off one another under normal conditions. But in the presence of a comb charged with static electricity they combine and become a single large drop."[27] The heavier the rain, the greater amount of electricity needed to collect the cloud droplets into rain drops. This is why during a heavy downpour there is a high amount of electrical activity, usually in the form of lightning.

---

[26]D. J. Malan, Physics of Lightning, (London, English Universities Press Ltd. 1963) p. 166.

[27]Philip D. Thompson, Robert O'Brien, "Weather", Life Science Library, (N. Y., Time, Inc., 1965) p. 103.

V
Physics

19. ALL MATTER AND ENERGY COMPLETED
AT UNIVERSE'S ORIGIN

Bible Writers: 1451 B.C.
Moses declared in Genesis 2:1,2, "Thus the heavens and the earth were completed, and all their hosts."

63 A.D.
Paul writes in Hebrews 4:3, "The works were finished from the foundation of the world."

ANALYSIS: The phrase, "all their hosts", which is the Hebrew expression "kal tsbaah", carries the meaning of "everything in them", or "everything therein." Thus Moses wrote that the heavens and the earth were complete, indicating that nothing, neither matter nor energy, has been needed or added since the time of the universe's origin.

FACT: Moses and Paul both attest to the fact that absolutely nothing has been added to the universe since it was "finished" at the time of its origin.

History of Science: Pre-1841 A.D.
Historical records show man's concept of the universe was never one of a closed, finished system after its origin. There was the constant strong belief in a continual creation, or the "spontaneous generation" of living things, and the disappearance into nothing of many objects.

1841 A.D.
Mayer formulated the law of mass and energy conservation which is also known as the First Law of Thermodynamics, and is considered the most important and basic law of all physical science. This law of energy conservation states that the sum total of all energy in the universe remains constant, but one form of energy may be converted into another.

A companion law is the law of mass conservation, which states that although matter may be changed in size, shape, form, etc., the total mass cannot be changed. These laws teach that NO Creation or Destruction of matter or energy is now being accomplished anywhere in the universe. They teach that the universe is functioning on that matter and power with which it originally began.

We have since learned that forms of energy and matter can be interchanged, but in the process, no new energy or matter is brought into, or taken out of, existence.

20. THE UNIVERSE IS DECAYING

Bible Writers: 745-695 B.C.
Isaiah 51:6, "Lift up your eyes to the sky, then look to the earth beneath; for the sky will vanish like smoke, and the earth will wear out like a garment, and its inhabitants will die in like manner."

538 B.C.
Psalms 102:26, speaks of the heavens and the earth: "Even they will perish, but Thou dost endure; and all of them will wear out like a garment."

63 A.D.
Hebrews 1:10,11 "Thou, Lord, in the beginning didst lay the foundation of the earth, and the heavens are the works of thy hands: they will perish, but Thou remainest; and they all will become old as a garment."

ANALYSIS: To "wear out like a garment" is to deteriorate or decay through age and use.

FACT: These writers picture the total universe as deteriorating through age from its original "finished" state.

History of Science: 1850 A.D.
The first indication science had that the universe was growing old and being used up, was the discovery of the Second Law of Thermodynamics, or as it is sometimes referred to, The Law of Entropy. This law is of almost as great a significance to science as the First Law of Thermodynamics.

This law of energy deterioration states that: in any energy transfer or change, although the total amount of energy remains unchanged, the amount of usefulness and availability that the energy possesses is always decreased. As the total of useless energy increases, the useful decreases by the same amount. This ratio of useless to useful energy is called "entropy". The Law of Entropy states that the ratio is constantly increasing and irreversible in flow. Since all activities of nature, including biological, physical, chemical, etc., involve energy transfers, there must be an ever decreasing supply of usable energy for maintaining the energizing processes in the universe.

An example of this deterioration is shown by use of the spectroscope in analyzing the sun. This study revealed that the hydrogen in the sun is being converted to helium at the rate of 4,600,000 tons per second in the process of producing radiant energy. "Eventually the sun must burn itself out, and then all activity on the earth must cease as well. The same principle applies to all the stars of the universe, so that the physical universe is beyond question, growing old, wearing out, and running down."[28]

Another proof of this "decaying" is that radioactive minerals are in a natural process of radioactive disintegration. As uranium and thorium disintegrate into other elements they yield great quantities of heat, which are radiated into space. This heat energy enters a state that can not be used by us again.

21. UNIVERSE BUILT OF THINGS NOT SEEN

Bible Writers: 63 A.D.
Hebrews 11:3, "By faith we understand that the worlds were prepared by the word of God, so that what is seen was not made out of the things which are visible."

Hebrews 1:3, ". . . upholding all things by the word of His power".

ANALYSIS: The word "things" is used in the Greek language to describe the smallest, most elementary, basic parts of anything. The letters of the alphabet are such "things" for our language.

The definition of the Greek word "dunamis" (Power) is inherent power, power residing in a thing by virtue of its nature. It is from this word we derive "dynamite" and "dynamo".

FACT: It was taught that "all things" are "upheld" and "hold together" by "inherent power", "so that what is

---

[28]Henry M. Morris, The Bible and Modern Science, (Chicago, Moody Press, 1951) p. 15.

seen was not made out of the things which are visible". In other words, the material of the universe is not ultimately physical, but composed of something which is not "apparent".

History of Science: 1895 A.D.
Roentgen began the modern era of atomic physics with the discovery of X-rays.

1923 A.D.
Men of past times have reasoned that all matter was built from visible things and could be completely and accurately described in terms of mechanical laws and models. As men's knowledge of matter grew through the development of instruments, it was learned that matter was divided into smaller and smaller particles. Whole molecules were seen using microscopes, then atoms. These atoms were thought to be the smallest division of matter until Dr. Robert Millikan developed an apparatus with which he isolated an electron. This discovery in 1923 won him the Nobel Physics award, and put the electron theory on a solid basis by devising a method for observing the charge of a single electron.

1970 A.D.
We have passed through the Electronic Age, Atomic Physics, Nuclear Physics, and are now entering what physicists call the age of Particle Physics. At Brookhaven, New York, the world's largest accelerator (atom smasher) accelerates protons to fantastic speeds and bombards various elements with these protons. This collision has caused heretofore unknown particles to break off the target atoms. New particles are being discovered at the rate of one every six weeks. Already the total of known particles is over one hundred. The

goal of modern physics is to discover a guiding principle that correlates all present knowledge about these unseen and yet to be explained entities.

Scientists now understand that all matter is held together by attraction and energy — things which are not apparent. In fact, the further science probes into matter, the more it is revealed that matter can be considered in terms of energy. For example, the actual matter in the human body would be smaller than the head of a pin.

22. LIGHT SPECTRUM

Bible Writers: 2000 B.C.
Job speaks of light in the following verses:
    Job 38:19, "Where is the way to the dwelling of light; and darkness, where is its place?"
    Job 38:24, "Where is the way that the light is divided?"

*ANALYSIS:*The Hebrew word for "way" is "derek".
The word carries not only the usage as related to "the way (path) to something", but also "the way (how) something is done". The first part of verse 19 literally translated from Hebrew reads, "What is the way (path where) the light dwells?" In verse 24 the word "way" would be "method", "or what manner" is light apportioned, or properly divided?

FACT: Job correctly stated the fact that light "dwells" in a "path", while darkness "exists" in a "place". He wrote that light could be "apportioned" and asked the question, "by what method?"

History of Science: 1675 A.D.
The fact that light was not an instantaneous transmission, but required a definite time to pass through space, and therefore exists in a path, was first discovered by Roemer in 1675. Now science knows, through its instruments, that light can dwell for millions of years in paths while traveling the path at the rate of 186,000 miles per second. Strangely enough, science does not know what light is, for neither the current "wave theory" nor the past "emission theory" can account for all the facts.

1666 A.D.
Sir Isaac Newton first demonstrated that light can be parted, or apportioned, when he discovered that a glass prism can be used to split a beam of light into bands of spectral colors. From this experiment came the instrument known as the spectroscope, although it was not until 1859 that its practical value was realized as a scientific tool. There is a field of science called Spectroscopy, which is built entirely around apportioning light.

VI
Biology

23. THREE KINGDOMS OF NATURAL SCIENCE

Bible Writers: 1491-1451 B.C.
The entire first chapter of Genesis as recorded by Moses.

Verse 3, "Let there be light"

9, "Let the waters under the heavens be gathered together unto one place, and let the dry land appear: and it was so"

11, "Let the earth sprout vegetation, plants yielding seed, and fruit trees bearing fruit after their kind, with seed in them, on the earth."

21, "And God created the great sea monsters, and every living creature that moves, with which the waters swarmed after their kind, and every winged bird after its kind."

24, "Then God said, 'Let the earth bring forth living creatures after their kind: cattle and creeping things and beasts of the earth after their kind; and it was so."

27, "And God created man in his own image"

ANALYSIS: Moses discusses origins by dividing the subject into three categories. The origin of minerals, verses 1-10; of the vegetable kingdom, verses 11-13; and the animal kingdom, verses 20-31.

FACT: The first chapter of Genesis is divided into the three kingdoms of natural science, and placed in their proper order for survival during the creation. The order of these kingdoms in Genesis is: mineral, vegetable, and animal.

History of Science: 1740 A.D.

No records of Babylon, Assyria, Egypt, or Greece show they knew such a division of nature. The division that was normally used was that between life and non-life. "It was finally Carolus Linnaeus, a Swedish botanist, who propounded the method and scheme of classification upon which all subsequent ones have been based".[29] He recognized that there are three basic kingdoms of natural science, and then chose to subdivide them into genera, and these he further subdivided into species as a fundamental unit of classification.

24. MAN AND WOMAN EACH HAVE SEED OF PROPAGATION

Bible Writers: 1491-1451 B.C.

Moses wrote of God speaking to Satan in Genesis 3:15, "And I will put enmity between you and the woman, and between your seed and her seed."

Moses also recorded in Genesis 13:15, God speaking to Abraham, "The land which you see, I will give it to you and to your descendants forever. And I will make your descendants as the dust of the earth; so that if anyone can number the dust of the earth, then your descendants can also be numbered."

---

[29]Chambers & Payne, From Cell to Test Tube, (N. Y., Charles Scribner's Son, 1960) p. 20.

63 A.D.
Paul wrote in Hebrews 7:9,10, "And, so to speak, through Abraham even Levi, who received tithes, paid tithes, for he was still in the loins of his father when Melchizedek met him."

ANALYSIS: The Bible's use of the word "seed" denotes the descendants generated by an individual's reproductive seed. In God's speech to Abraham the word "descendant" is derived from the word "seed" in the Hebrew. An example of the male having seed is the reference to Levi who descended and lived 400 years after Abraham.

FACT: Moses revealed that both men and women had "seed" necessary for child bearing.

History of Science: 1000 A.D.
To this time it had been universally accepted that only the males of a species had the seed of propagation. Michael Psellos, who lived in Constantinople during the 11th Century is the first recorded to believe both male and female contributed semen to a born embryo.[30]

1451-1519 A.D.
Leonardo da Vinci was ahead of his time when he observed, "If black gets black with child, the offspring is black; but if a black gets white with child the offspring is gray. And this shows that the seed of the mother has power in the embryo equally with that of the father."[31]

---

[30]Sirlas & Zirkle, Evolution of Biology (N. Y., Ronald Press Co., 1964) p. 93.
[31]Ibid — Note 1, p. 124.

1600 A.D.
"Before the invention of the microscope, observations on development were of the most superficial sort and the genesis of the organism from the egg was chiefly a problem for the philosopher."[32]During the 17th and 18th centuries the theory known as "preformation" was the dominant view. According to this theory nothing new arises, but each germ or seed must contain in diminishing series the germs of all succeeding generations. This is known as the "box-within-box theory". Naturally, most of the preformationists believed the germ to be contained in the female egg.

1677 A.D.
The discovery, via the microscope, of spermatozoa by Hamm caused the rise of a new theory known as the "spermists", who adopted the view that these minute living bodies carried the germs, and therefore the egg was merely a fertilizer.

1880 A.D.
"It was 1880 before establishment of the equality of the female ovum with the male spermatozoon, thus ending the prolonged battle between the spermatists and ovists (preformationists)."[33] At this point in time, science resolved the philosophical arguments about the reproduction of human life by proving both parties wrong. Both men and women have seed of propagation.

---

[32]J. H. McGregor, "Embryology", Encyclopedia Americana, Vol. 10, 1957 ed. p. 277.
[33]Op. Cit. — Note 1, p. 93.

25. ALL ANIMALS REPRODUCE AFTER THEIR OWN KIND

Bible Writers: 1491-1451 B.C.
Moses again recorded in Genesis 1:21,24,25, "God created the great sea-monsters, and every living creature that moves, with which the waters swarmed, after their kind, and every winged bird after its kind; . . . Then God said, 'Let the earth bring forth living creatures after their kind: cattle and creeping things and beasts of the earth after their kind'; and it was so. And God made the beasts of the earth after their kind, and the cattle after their kind, and everything that creeps on the ground after its kind."

Genesis 6:19,20, "Of every living thing of all flesh, you shall bring two of every kind into the ark, to keep them alive with you; they shall be male and female. Of the birds after their kind, and of the animals after their kind, of every creeping thing of the ground after its kind."

ANALYSIS: The Hebrew meaning for "kind" or "sort" is considered the basic divisions of animal life, relative to the term genera, family, or order.

FACT: Moses considered it fact that "every living creature that moves", whether in the "waters" or "birds", or "beasts", or the things that "creep", "multiplied after its own kind", and there is both "male and female" of "every living thing".

History of Science: 350 B.C.
All Greek philosophers held with the Aristotlian dictum that "eggs" of all lower animals are formed out of rotting substances. It was out of this corruption that insects originated. Frogs and other small sealife had

their origin in slime pools or sea water. This idea which persisted for centuries became known as the "Spontaneous Generation Theory".

1626-1698 A.D.

An Italian, Francesco Redi, disproved that spontaneous generation applied to insects. He saw flies were attracted to rotten meat, so he covered some with parchment and left some open in pans. He observed flies were attracted to both. No eggs were on the parchment even though the smell came through and attracted flies. Eggs did appear on the open meat and thus maggots came out. Therefore Redi concluded flies come only from matched eggs of other flies. Subsequently the theory was limited to the microbes Leeuwenhoek found through his invention of the microscope in 1676.

1862 A.D.

Louis Pasteur won first prize from the French Academie des Sciences in 1862 for the project defined: "Attempt by means well devised, experiments to throw new light on the question of spontaneous generation". His research efforts proved once and for all that there is no spontaneous generation, but that all living things are a product of living matter.

1900 A.D.

At the beginning of the 17th century Europe still believed in hybridized animals. These were the supposed intermixing through mating between species. Weird offspring were reported to have been seen by learned men in remote places, and some animals such as the hyena, were believed to change their sex every year.

Mendel's Law, the law of heredity discovered by Johann Gergot Mendel, was first published in 1865, although it was overlooked until attention was called to his remarkable results by De Vries in 1900.

Mendel's Law proved that offspring inherit, produce, and exhibit the characteristics of the parents according to dominant and recessive characteristics. This makes possible the breeding of a great variety within a species, and eliminated the belief in hybridized animals. The law is based on the fact that the sperm of the male carries all the ancestry of the male, and the ovum the same for the female. What is done to change variety has to be done to the genes which carry the specific physical differences.

Each genera, or "kind", has a different number of self-perpetuating chromosomes and cannot be intermated with another. We now know the human cell has 46 chromosomes, with each parent providing 23 toward the makeup of their offspring. Thus all living things perpetuate their "likeness" through their offspring.

26. ALL FLESH IS NOT THE SAME

Bible Writers: 56 A.D.
The apostle Paul wrote in 1 Corinthians 15:39, "All flesh is not the same flesh; but there is one flesh of men, and another flesh of beasts, and another flesh of birds, and another of fish."

ANALYSIS: The word "flesh" in Hebrew denotes "meat".

FACT: Paul noted that all flesh is not the same and recorded four types: men, beasts, birds and fish.

History of Science: 1838 A.D.

Men had always held that flesh, or meats, were for the most part the same. Matthias J. Schleiden (1838) and especially Theodor Schwann (1839) established the cell theory, recognizing the cell as a unit of structure in both plants and animals. Having only the use of the light microscope, these men and their contemporaries could not make close and accurate observations of individual cells. Their conclusion, therefore, stated that all cells were identical and did not originate from other cells. This "common cell theory" was held for years. This cell was considered to be the common building block of all life, thus giving further argument to the theory all flesh is the same. It was argued that all meat had the same construction, built of these common cells.

1930 A.D.

It took the invention of the electron microscope in early 1930's to give science the tool it needed to look into cell structure. H. Busch in 1926 invented the principle for operation of this instrument. The best light microscope could not reveal structure below 1/100,000 of an inch. The electron microscope will enlarge over this one-hundred times. The work done with this instrument, plus improved killing fluids, and machines that slice cells into sections, revised the theory of cell continuity. Individual cell structure can now be shown clearly. There were discovered to be many different types rather than one basic cell. These differ radically in structure, chemical composition, methods of eating, methods of reproduction, and purpose. A piece of flesh can now be analyzed accurately enough to tell its species. The latest combination light-electron microscope can focus images to 1/2,000,000 of an inch, thus defining the differences even more clearly.

It is interesting to note that modern science's division of animal life is man, beast, fish, and fowl.

27. WATERS SWARM WITH SWARMS OF LIVING CREATURES

BIBLE Writers: 1491-1451 B.C.
Moses stated in Genesis 1:20 that, "The waters teem with swarms of living creatures."

ANALYSIS: The translated meaning of "creatures", the Hebrew word "sherets", is rapidly multiplying active mass of minute animals.

FACT: Moses revealed that "waters teem with swarms of living rapidly multiplying minute animals".

History of Science: 1676 A.D.
Leeuwenhoek's hobby was grinding bits of glass into powerful lenses. In his attic laboratory he perfected the technique so that he was able to magnify objects as much as 270 times. Constantly curious, he caught some rain water and looking at a drop through his microscope, could not believe what he saw. He called to his daughter, "See what I see, Maria. There are little animals in this rain water."

It was not until this development of the microscope by Leeuwenhoek that man could see "waters swarming with swarms of living rapidly multiplying creatures". No sea life known or recorded of man had ever been described as such, until the eye viewed water aided by a microscope. In fact, it would be difficult to better portray what is seen in water through a powerful microscope.

Every drop of water in plant, spring, or animal contains colonies of life. A typical example would be protozoa spores which dry up and are in the air, earth, etc. When they become wet they come to life and will hatch. One species lives sixty hours, matures in twelve and reproduces an average of sixty young every twelve hours. At the death of the parents they would have 55,411,260 descendants.

28. LIFE IS IN THE BLOOD

Bible Writers: 1491-1451 B.C.
Moses wrote in Leviticus 17:11, "The life of the flesh is in the blood."

ANALYSIS: The Hebrew definition for "life" is "that which makes it possible for an animal to breathe; also vitality".

FACT: Moses pronounced that "the life of the flesh is in the blood".

History of Science: 350 B.C.
Blood letting is known to have been practiced as early as the 4th century B.C. Herophilos, a physician of the Museum at Alexandria, advocated it as a means to rid the body of disease. Many of his contemporaries also used it as a cure, considering blood a carrier of DISEASE instead of LIFE.

1616 A.D.
This practice was later based on the theory that blood would ebb and flow, with new blood being created rapidly. The monumental discovery by William Harvey, a British physician, in 1616 that blood circulated continually through the veins to be used over and over again has enabled man to make exact studies of the circulation system and the function of blood.

1800 A.D.

The barber-surgeons of this country were the professional blood letters until the early 19th century, hence the origin of the red stripe on their poles. A conscientious barber-surgeon would bleed a person, to free him of disease, from both arms so as supposedly not to off balance his weight. This was often done while trimming the patient's hair.

1900 A.D.

The pre-eminent importance of the blood in the biological mechanism has only been comprehended with any adequacy in recent years. In this century scientists have discovered that the continuance of life depends upon the continued temperature control, waste removal, and transportation of water, food and regulators to the cells of all parts of the body, and therefore the very life and nourishment of the body are furnished by the blood.

29. MANKIND IS OF ONE ORIGIN

Bible Writers: 63 A.D.

Luke quoted Paul as speaking of God in Acts 17:26, "He made of one every nation of mankind to live on all the face of the earth."

FACT: Paul revealed that men of every nation are of one origin.

History of Science: 1775 A.D.

Until this time there were considered to be five distinct original races based on skin color as outlined by Johann Friedrich Blumenback, the founder of Anthropology. These races were considered to be perpetuated by the differences in the blood of each. Although later anthropologists developed other systems to determine original races, such as characteristics of the body, languages, location, etc., few could agree as to what and how many original pure races there were.

1900 A.D.
In 1900 Karl Landsteiner discovered that all human blood has one common base, plasma. Blood can be divided into four basic types, differing in the types of cells carried in the plasma. Comparative studies of people in different lands have shown that human populations all over the world contain almost equal proportions of the four blood types.

The race concept of classical anthropology and biology proved unsatisfactory because it was based on the "blood line" theory of inheritance, which assumes that heredity is transmitted from parents to offspring through blood. "Although this theory was invalidated by the discovery of Mendel's Laws of heredity it continues to be credited almost universally by laymen, and even colors the thinking of some scientists."[34] As already noted, modern genetics show that heredity is transmitted through discrete genes.

It is now scientifically evident that all races of men are biologically similar, so that all known variations in mankind are possible within the human cell structure. As already noted, the human cell with its 46 chromosomes differs completely from every other living thing. Therefore, applying Mendel's law of the offspring inheriting the characteristics only of its ancestors, most scientists conclude that all men have one common ancestor.

[34]Dobzhansky, "Races, Nature, and Origins Of", Encyclopedia Americana, Vol. 23, 1957 ed., p. 109.

30. HEALTH AND SANITATION

Bible Writers: 1491-1451 B.C.
Moses recorded many laws regarding health and sanitation for the Jewish nation. For the purpose of examination, Moses' writings will be divided into the following three categories:

I.   Food Contamination from the book of Leviticus,

    A. 11:32-40, "Anything on which one of them may fall when they are dead, becomes unclean, including any wooden article, or clothing, or a skin, or a sack — any article of which use is made — it shall be put in the water and be unclean until evening, then it becomes clean. As for any earthenware vessel into which one of them may fall, whatever is in it becomes unclean and you shall break the vessel. Any of the food which may be eaten on which water comes shall become unclean; and any liquid which may be drunk in every vessel shall become unclean. Everything, moreover, on which part of their carcass may fall becomes unclean; an oven or a store shall be smashed; they are unclean and shall continue as unclean to you. Nevertheless a spring or a cistern collecting water shall be clean, though the one who touches their carcass shall be unclean. And if a part of their carcass falls on any seed for sowing which is to be sown, it is clean. Though if water is put on the seed, and a part of their carcass falls on it, it is unclean to you. Also if one of the animals dies which you have for food, the one who touches its carcass becomes unclean until evening. He too, who eats some of its carcass shall wash his clothes and be unclean until evening; and the one who picks up its carcass shall wash his clothes and be unclean until evening."

B. 7:19, "Also the flesh that touches anything unclean shall not be eaten; it shall be burned with fire."

C. 7:26, "And you are not to eat any blood, either of bird or animal, in any of your dwellings."

II. Sanitation

A. Leviticus 17:13b, "When any man . . . in hunting catches a beast or a bird which may be eaten, he shall pour out its blood and cover it with earth."

B. Deuteronomy 23:12,13, "You shall also have a place outside the camp and go out there, and you shall have a spade among your tools, and it shall be when you sit down outside, you shall dig with it and shall turn to cover up your excrement."

III. Sickness

A. Leviticus, chapters 13 and 14 contain the laws for identification, isolation, and control of leprosy.

13:14-17, "But whenever raw flesh appears on him, he shall be unclean. And the priest shall look at the raw flesh, and he shall pronounce him unclean; the raw flesh is unclean, it is leprosy. Or if the raw flesh turns again and is changed to white, then shall he come to the priest, and the priest shall look at him, and behold, if the infection has turned to white, then the priest shall pronounce clean him who has the infection; he is clean."

13:45,46, "As for the leper who has the infection, his clothes shall be torn, and the hair of his head shall be uncovered, and he shall cover his mustache and cry Unclean! Unclean! He shall remain unclean all the days during which he has the infection; he is unclean. He shall live alone; his dwelling shall be outsidè the camp."

13:52, So he shall burn the garment, whether the warp of the woof, in wool or linen, or any article of leather in which the mark occurs, for it is a leprous malignancy; it shall be burned in the fire."

14:8,9, "The one to be cleansed shall then wash his clothes and shave off all his hair, and bathe in water and be clean. Now afterward, he may enter the camp, but he shall stay outside his tent for seven days. And it will be on the seventh day that he shall shave off all his hair: he shall shave his head and his beard and his eyebrows, even all his hair. He shall then wash his clothes and bathe his body in water and be clean."

14:39-47, "And the priest shall return on the seventh day and make an inspection. If the mark has indeed spread in the walls of the house, then the priest shall order them to tear out the stones with the mark in them and throw them away at an unclean place outside the city. And he shall have the house scraped all around inside, and they shall dump the plaster that they scrape off at an unclean place outside the city. Then they shall take other stones and replace those stones; and he shall take other plaster and replaster the house. If, however, the mark breaks out again in the house, after he has torn out the stones and scraped the house, and after it has been replastered, then the priest shall come in and make an inspection. If he sees that the mark has indeed spread in the house, it is a malignant mark in the house; it is unclean. He shall therefore tear down the house, its stones, and its timbers, and all the plaster of the house, and he shall take them outside the city to an unclean place. Moreover, whoever goes into the house during the time that he has quarantined it, becomes unclean until evening. Likewise, whoever lies down in the house shall wash his clothes, and whoever eats in the house shall wash his clothes."

B. Leviticus, chapter 15 provides laws concerning those individuals who have running issues of fluids that come from the body.

15:7,8, "Also whoever touches the person with the discharge shall wash his clothes and bathe in water and be unclean until evening. Or if the man with the discharge spits on one who is clean, he too shall wash his clothes and bathe in water and be unclean until evening."

15:11-13, "Likewise, whomever the one with the discharge touches without having rinsed his hands in water shall wash his clothes and bathe in water and be unclean until evening. However, an earthenware vessel which the person with the discharge touches shall be broken, and every wooden vessel shall be rinsed in water. Now when the man with the discharge becomes cleansed from his discharge, then he shall count off for himself seven days for his cleansing; he shall then wash his clothes and bathe his body in running water and shall become clean."

ANALYSIS:

I. Under food contamination Moses gave the following restrictions:

   A. When rodents, lizards, or creeping things died and touched any implement, vessel, or raiment, the things made from earth or clay were to be destroyed while the rest could be washed in water to be made clean.

   B. When that classified as "unclean" touched food or drink, the meat was to be burned, drink poured out, and the rest properly disposed of.

   C. He forbade them to eat the blood of any animal, which included the proper bleeding of animals at their death and the disposal of the blood.

II. Laws of Sanitation called for the burial of animal blood and human excreta.

III. Moses gave comprehensive laws concerning sickness. These included laws for those having leprosy or cases with open sores or skin lesions.

   A. Recognition of infected individuals.

   B. Quarantine or isolation.

   C. The wearing of a mask over the mouth and nose.

   D. The "uncleanness" of anything touched by these people.

   E. To "clean" oneself included bathing of the body and clothes in running water, and in some cases the removal of all body hair first.

   F. When garments and buildings show signs that the disease cannot be arrested, then that portion or all of the object should be destroyed and removed from town.

FACT: Moses recorded laws comparable to modern health and sanitation practice in most civilized countries.

History of Science: 1350 A.D.
The word "quarantine" originated when the Italian ports of Venice and Genoa first refused admission to immigrants who might be harboring plague and required them to stay on board for forty days.

1676 A.D.
The beginning of microbiology began when Leeuwenhoek invented the microscope and in the same year published his discovery.

1700 A.D.
Leprosy spread over southern Europe in the seventeenth and eighteenth centuries until the principles of Moses were re-enacted successfully.[35]

1855 A.D.
Pasteur, in experimenting with molds, discovered bacteria thus ushering into science the significant field of bacteriology.

1892 A.D.
"Conclusive evidence of the actual existence of such infectious matter (viral) dates only from 1892."[36]Louis Pasteur was one of the first to use the information. Men can now give scientific reasons for a nation adopting the strict health code that Moses decreed.

1930 A.D.
Doctors now tell us that the eating of blood can transmit disease. It is also a health law in most countries that no animal may be butchered for food that is not slain and bled properly.

---

[35]R. William, "Medical Science and the Bible", Modern Science and the Christian Faith (Chicago: Scripture Press), 1948, p. 244.
[36]Sirlas and Zirkle, Evolution of Biology, Op. Cit., p. 273.

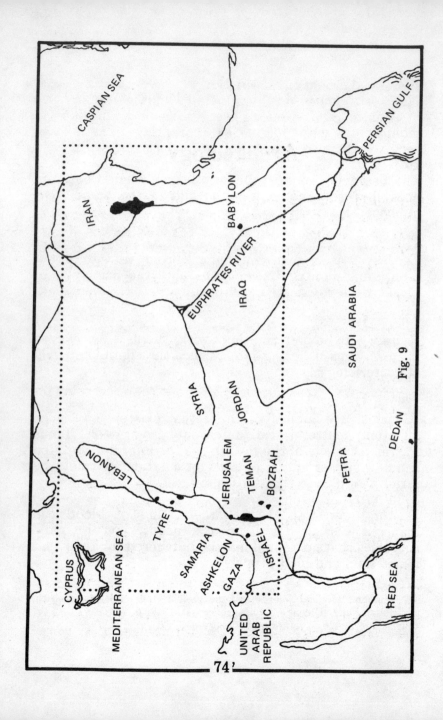

Fig. 9

74

VII
Archaeology

Our world is dotted with the sites of ancient cities that are found recorded in the Bible. These archaeological sites give visible testimony for the inspiration of the Biblical writers. Their writings contain many prophecies of God directed toward some of the important cities of their time. Now we have very old copies of their prophetic writings, such as the Dead Sea Scrolls, which are known to have existed long before the fulfillment of these prophecies actually occurred and they became events of history. Yes, these are provable facts today. They stand as indisputable monuments to the Bible's inspiration.

Archaeological expeditions have explored the ruins of ancient cities with the consistant result of proving the historical and prophetic accuracy of the Bible writers. It is true that some prophecies cannot now be proven to have been written either before or after the actual event spoken of occurred. But, what is the "modernist" doing with those which can be proven true prophecies? He is observed doing the same as men did nineteen centuries ago when some, who witnessed the very miracles of Jesus, rejected the obvious conclusion of this evidence because of their pride, jealousy, position, etc.

The ability to prophesy is a definite test of man's inspiration. "Let them bring forth, and declare to us what is going to take place; . . . or announce to us what is coming. Declare the things that are going to come afterward, that we may know that you are gods."[37]No prophecy was ever made by an act of human will, but men moved by the Holy Spirit spoke from God.[38]No more tangible proof could be provided that there IS a God, than for Him to declare what He will do long before He does it; and that in written records. Then, centuries after the world had copies of these declarations, He caused the specific events to happen precisely as He stated.

"Thus says the Lord, the King of Israel and his Redeemer, the Lord of hosts: 'I am the first and I am the last, and there is no God besides Me. And who is like Me? Let him proclaim it; yes, let him recount it to Me in order, from the time that I established the ancient people. And let them declare to them the things that are coming and the events that are going to take place. Do not tremble and do not be afraid; have I not long since announced it to you and declared it? And you are My witnesses. Is there any God besides Me, or is there any other Rock? I know of none.'"[39] The early Christians used prophecy to sustain and prove that their religion was from God. We also have the same obligation to the world today. You must "always be ready to make a defense to every one who asks you to give an account for the hope that is in you."[40]

31. CITY OF SAMARIA

Bible Writers: 750 B.C.
Micah 1:6, "For I will make Samaria a heap of ruins in the open country, planting places for a vineyard. I will

[37]Isaiah 41:22, 23.
[38]2 Peter 1:21.
[39]Isaiah 44:6-8.
[40]1 Peter 2:15.

76

pour her stones down into the valley, and will lay bare her foundations.

FACT: Prophetic events concerning the city of Samaria summarized:

1. Its ruins would become as a "heap of the field". Places within the city would be cleared of ruins and debris would be gathered into piles, similar to the "heaps" created in the clearing of farm land.
2. In clearing the site, the building stones would be pushed off the terraces into the valley below.
3. Even the foundations of buildings and road beds would be dug up in an effort to clear land for planting.
4. Eventually Samaria would be planted in vineyards.

History: 880 B.C.
The city of Samaria was built as the capital of the northern kingdom of Israel. King Omri built it on isolated Mt. Sameron which is completely surrounded by an almost circular valley. Mt. Sameron was terraced around from the valley floor to about the 400 foot elevation for building sites.

27 B.C.
Herod the Great beautified the city including the construction of palaces and temples.

1265 A.D.
Moslems defeated the Crusaders defending the city and totally destroyed it, so that it has never been rebuilt. Arabs living in the vicinity cleared much of the ruins to convert the ancient city's site to agricultural purposes. In clearing the land they dug up building foundations and roadways, either piling the rubble in heaps, or

dumping it down to the lower terraces, and eventually to the valley floor. See Photo 1 where the site of Ahab's Palace is being excavated.

Today
On the second terrace from the top there stand the remaining pillars of a colonnade built by Herod the Great, which once extended around the hill for a distance of 1000 yards. Now grape vines and olive trees can be seen growing in many clearings, including the roadway between the columns, as seen in Photo 2.
NOTE: Usually ancient cities were built upon the ruins of their predecessor. After rebuilding Samaria eight times, God stopped the rebuilding and caused the site to be converted back to agriculture.

32. CITIES OF EDOM

Bible Writers: 600 B.C.
Jeremiah 49:13,17, "Bozrah will become an object of horror, a reproach, a ruin and a curse; and all its cities will become perpetual ruins. ... And Edom will become an object of horror; everyone who passes by it will be horrified and will hiss at all its wounds."

500 B.C.
Ezekiel 25:13, "Thus says the Lord God, 'I will also stretch out My hand against Edom and cut off man and beast from it. And I will lay it waste; from Teman even to Dedan they will fall by the sword.'"

Ezekiel 35:3,4,7, and 9, "Behold, I am against you, Mount Seir, and I will stretch out My hand against you, and will make you a desolation and a waste. I will lay waste your cities, and you will become a desolation. ... And I will make Mount Seir a waste and a desolation, and will cut off from it the one who passes through and returns. . . . I will make you an everlasting desolation, and your cities will not be inhabited. Then you will know that I am the Lord."

FACT: Prophecy concerning the cities of Edom summarized.

1. The cities of Edom laying in the Seir Mountain Range would become a perpetual desolation from the city of Teman in the North, to Dedan in the South, including Bozrah the capital.
2. The ruins would become an astonishment to those who viewed them.
3. The ancient famous caravan route along the King's Highway, which used these cities as trading places and stations, would cease.

History: 300 A.D.
The trade route, which was of great importance, along the King's Highway between Syria and Arabia shifted north on a new highway through the city of Palmyra.

632 A.D.
The once strong city of Petra was conquered and destroyed by Mohammedans and disappeared from the annals of human history with even its site unknown.

1188 A.D.
The remaining original cities of Edom lying between Teman and Dedan fell in 1188 before the armies of Arab Saracen Saladin and were left wasted and in ruins.

1812 A.D.
The now famous ruins of Petra were discovered in 1812 by Burchardt, and, because of their state of preservation, are one of the most astonishing archaeological sites

Photo 1

Photo 2

Photo 3

known; see Photo 3. Expeditions have located most of the sites of the other cities.

Today
All the ancient cities of Edom located in Mount Seir have stood desolate for centuries; see Photo 4.
NOTE: These silent sites remain as perpetual astonishments. Like dead men's bones, intentionally unburied, lying bleaching in the sun. They forever remain a testimony to the living, from God, of a past people who were destroyed for their wickedness.

33. CITIES OF GAZA AND ASHKELON

Bible Writers: 800 B.C.
Amos 1:8, " 'The remnant of the Philistines will perish,' says the Lord God."

630 B.C.
Zephaniah 2:4,6, "For Gaza will be abandoned, and Ashkelon a desolation; . . . So the seacoast will be pastures, with caves for shepherds and folds for flocks."

600 B.C.
Jeremiah 47:5, "Baldness has come upon Gaza; Ashkelon has been ruined."

FACT: Prophecy concerning the cities of Gaza and Ashkelon summarized.
1. The Philistines, as a people, would perish.
2. One of their capital cities, Gaza, would be forsaken and "baldness" would come upon it.
3. Ashkelon, another of their capital cities, would also become desolate. But, it and its sea-coast would

81

become the dwelling place of shepherds with their sheep folds.

History: 600 B.C.
These prophecies were made when the Philistines were one of the most powerful nations in the area. The name "Palestine" means, "Land of Philistines".

96 B.C.
The Maccabees of Israel, led by Alexander Jannaeus, completely exterminated the Philistines in a series of seventeen battles.

1270 A.D.
Ashkelon had existed for over 2500 years as a major coastal city. Herod the Great had built a large summer resort there. This city was destroyed by Sulton Bibars in 1270 A.D. and has never been rebuilt.

1921 A.D.
Old Gaza was found by an archaeological exploration group buried under a large dune of sand along the Mediterranean coast.

Today
The Philistines are the only ancient race of people of the area, from among about twenty races, that were so completely destroyed that they have no descendants among today's nations.

Today the vicinity of Ashkelon no longer has the traditional grain fields, but shepherds use the remains of old structures to build sheep folds and shepherd hovels; see Photo 5. The city and its sea-coast are otherwise desolate.

Photo 4

Photo 5

Photo 6

Gaza truly remains desolate being completely covered with sand. Such a dune of sand is a fitting description for, "baldness has come upon Gaza"; see Photo 6.
NOTE: The most troublesome people to ancient Israel were the Philistines. Now, among all the former races, they alone have disappeared. Out of the five major Philistine capitals, one has become a large sand dune, one deserted and salvaged for pasture fences and hovels, while the remaining three are populated today with another people. The prophetic accuracy is phenomenal!

34. CITY OF BABYLON

Bible Writers: 700 B.C.
Isaiah 13:19-22, "And Babylon, the beauty of kingdoms, the glory of the Chaldean's pride, will be as when God overthrew Sodom and Gomorrah. It will never be inhabited or lived in from generation to generation; nor will the Arab pitch his tent there, nor will shepherds make their flocks lie down there. But desert creatures will lie down there, and their houses will be full of owls, ostriches also will live there, and shaggy goats will frolic there. And hyenas will howl in their fortified towers and jackals in their luxurious palaces."

Isaiah 14:23, "I will also make it a possession for the hedgehog, and swamps of water, and I will sweep it with the broom of destruction."

Isaiah 25:12, "And the unassailable fortifications of your walls He will bring down, lay low, and cast to the ground, even to the dust."

600 B.C.
Jeremiah 50:12,13, "Behold, she shall be the least of the nations, a wilderness, a dry land, and a desert. Because

of the wrath of Jehovah she shall not be inhabited, but she shall be wholly desolate."

Jeremiah 51:25,26, "Behold, I am against you, O destroying mountain, . . . and I will make you a burnt out mountain. And they will not take from you even a stone for a corner nor a stone for foundations, but you will be desolate forever, declares the Lord."

Jeremiah 51:36,37, and 42, "And I shall dry up her sea and make her mountain dry. And Babylon will become a heap of ruins, a haunt of jackals, an object of horror and hissing, without inhabitants. . . . The sea has come up over Babylon; she has been engulfed with its tumultuous waves. Her cities have become an object of horror, a parched land and desert, a land in which no man lives."

FACT: Prophecy concerning the city of Babylon summarized.

1. The city of Babylon would become ruins and be perpetually uninhabited. The Arabian would not make his camp there nor graze sheep there, and the caravans would not pass through it.
2. Wild beasts would live in their palaces and houses.
3. Its protective moat, a man-made sea extending the Euphrates River from the walls up to a distance of 64 miles, would become dry; yet pools of water would cover portions of the city within the walls.
4. Her stones would not be taken for other buildings, but she would become heaps, the walls broken down, and the ziggurat burned, the famous "Hanging Gardens" on the man-made mountain of stone, known as one of the seven wonders of the world destroyed.
5. Babylon would remain a perpetual desolation and astonishment.

6. Her exceedingly fertile valley would become a dry parched wilderness and desert.

History: 100 A.D.
Due to several previous centuries' lack of sufficient rain, the Euphrates River became saline. This river-borne salt eventually destroyed the fertility of the land about the city of Babylon, and the city dwindled in population.

412 A.D.
The elaborate network of canals built to assure great productivity and to control flooding of the Euphrates River had become filled in due to lack of maintenance, thus causing the whole area to become swampy.

460 A.D.
Theodoret writes that by this time there were no longer any Assyrians or Chaldeans living there, only a few Jews.

1000 A.D.
The Euphrates River changed its course from the canal passing through the center of the city to a new route many miles to the east, thus causing the man-made sea to dry up.

1250 A.D.
Benjamin of Tudela visited the site and found nothing but utter desolation. Because of infestation by scorpions and serpents the palace proved to be inaccessible.

Today
The city of Babylon is desolate, except for wild animals that can be seen living among the ruins. As the walls of

the buildings in the city deteriorated, the mortar caused the soil to be tainted with nitrous compounds that poison the soil. Due to the soils' deterioration, and local superstition, the Arabs will not camp nor graze flocks near the ancient city. For over 4000 years it was on a major trade route, but no longer.

Babylon is acclaimed to be the oldest and the most beautiful city the world has had. It now lies stripped of its life and beauty. Other than normal erosion and weathering, the city exists today with its bridges, buildings, and walls as it did 2000 years ago. The walls, which once stood 300 feet high and 80 to 120 feet thick, were made out of brick, and are weathered down completely in places; see Photo 7. The stones of the famous ziggurat still show signs of having been burned with intensive heat. The building materials of the city were not removed and used again, as is customary; see Photo 8.

Over the centuries the rising water table in the plain has rendered much of the remains of earlier centuries inaccessible by causing one quarter of the city to be under pools of water and swamps.

A small tourist hotel, run by the Syrian government, caters to those who venture into this now desolate land to see the famous ruins of the 14 mile square city of antiquity.

NOTE: The fall of the greatest, most splendid and oldest city in the world attests to the exactness of God's prophecies. Alexander the Great attempted to rebuild the city and died there. Having become completely desolate, it remains as a monument of God's providence in the affairs of men. If God caused the strongest nation known till modern times to fall in one night, then he can do the same again to any nation that grows in sin.

Photo 7

Photo 8

35. CITY OF TYRE

Bible Writers: 550 B.C.

Ezekiel 26:3-5, "Thus says the Lord God, 'Behold I am against you, O Tyre, and I will bring up many nations against you, as the sea brings up its waves. And they will destroy the walls of Tyre and break down her towers; and I will scrape her debris from her and make her a bare rock. She will be a place for the spreading of nets in the midst of the sea, for I have spoken,' declares the Lord God."

Photo 9

Photo·10

Ezekiel 26:12,14, and 21, " 'They will make spoil of your riches and a prey of your merchandise, break down your walls and destroy your pleasant houses, and throw your stones and your timbers and your debris into the water. . . . And I will make you a bare rock; you will be a place for the spreading of nets. You will be built no more, for I the Lord have spoken, . . . I shall bring terrors on you, and you will be found no more: though you will be sought, you will never be found again,' declares the Lord God."

FACT: Prophecy concerning the city of Tyre summarized.

1. Many nations, as waves of the sea, would come against Tyre.
2. The walls and buildings would be torn down and cast into the water. All the stone, timber, and even the soil down to bedrock, would be covered by the sea.
3. The city site would be made a bare rock and used as a place for the spreading and repair of fishing nets.
4. The city of Tyre would no longer exist or be found.

History: 586 B.C.

The rich and famous city of the seafaring Phoenicians, Tyre, came under siege by Nebuchadnezzar, king of Babylon. After thirteen years of land siege, the Phoenicians built a second and smaller city on an island one half mile out in the Mediterranean Sea. Using their ships, they removed themselves from the threat of the Babylonian Empire, leaving their once beautiful capital stripped and deserted. Its ruins seem to contest Ezekiel's prophecy. Who would be foolish enough to throw all the city's debris and soil into the sea? What use would such an undertaking be?

322 B.C.

Alexander the Great conquered the coastal cities to acquire their navies, and sent them against the new city of Tyre in constant waves. Judging this procedure too slow, he had his army build a causeway the width of two chariots from the shore of the old city to the island of the new Tyre. He ordered all building materials from the original city to be collected and placed in the sea to make this causeway. When the quantity of stone and timber proved insufficient, he ordered the ground scraped down to bedrock to provide fill dirt, and thus finished the causeway. He then marched his army over the causeway to defeat the Phoenicians and destroy their new city, ending his seven month seige.

Today

The city the prophets spoke against for God is now a large bare rock. For centuries the site has been used by fishermen to spread and mend their nets; see Photo 9. The stone, timbers, and dirt of that city lie in the water with part of the causeway still visible; see Photo 10.

Other than historical records, there is no evidence that one of the world's richest cities ever existed. It can never be found again.

NOTE: A nation strong enough to withstand the siege of mighty Babylon was brought down through a series of specific events that had been foretold by Prophets. Today about 5,000 descendants live on the backside of the island in shacks, while the ancient site of their once famous capital is strewn with everpresent fishing nets.

VIII
The Bible

If the preceding pages convinced you that the ancient Bible writers obtained information beyond their human ability, then you will be interested in their account of this information's origin which follows.

GOD

INHERENT AUTHORITY because He is the universe's originator.

Genesis 1:1, "In the beginning God created the heavens and the earth."

DELEGATED AUTHORITY from God.

CHRIST

Matthew 28:18, "All authority has been given to me in heaven and on earth."

I Corinthians 15:27, "He has put all things in subjection under His feet. But when He says, 'All things are put in subjection,' it is evident that He is excepted who put all things in subjection to Him."

HOLY SPIRIT

GUIDED AND GUARDED Apostles.

John 14:26, "The Holy Spirit, whom the Father will send in my name, he shall teach you all things, and bring to your remembrance all that I said to you."

John 16:13, "But when He, the Spirit of truth, comes, He will guide you into all the truth; for He will not speak on His own initiative, but whatever He hears, He will speak; and He will disclose to you what is to come. He shall glorify Me, for He shall take of Mine, and shall disclose it to you. All things that the Father has are Mine; therefore I said, that He takes of Mine, and will disclose it to you."

I Corinthians 2:10-13, "For to us God revealed them through the Spirit; for the Spirit searches all things, even the depths of God. For who among men knows the thoughts of a man except the spirit of the man, which is in him? Even so the thoughts of God no one knows except the Spirit of God. Now we have received not the spirit of the world, but the Spirit who is from God, that we might know the things freely given to us by God, which things we also speak, not in words taught by human wisdom, but in those taught by the Spirit, combining spiritual thoughts with spiritual words."

APOSTLE

DELEGATED AUTHORITY from Christ.

John 17:8, Jesus said, "For the words which thou gavest me I have given unto them."

John 20:21, "Jesus therefore said to them . . . As the father has sent me, even so send I you."

John 13:20, Jesus said, "Truly, truly, I say to you, he who receives whomever I send receives Me; and he who receives Me receives Him who sent Me."

Galatians 1:11,12, "For I would have you know, brethren, that the gospel which was preached by me is not according to man. For I neither received it from man, nor was I taught it, but I received it through a revelation of Jesus Christ."

BIBLE

WRITTEN by the Apostles and Prophets.

Ephesians 3:3-5, Paul said, "By revelation there was made known to me the mystery, as I wrote before in brief. And by referring to this, when you read you can understand my insight into the mystery of Christ, which in other generations was not made known to the sons of men, as it has now been revealed to His holy apostles and prophets in the Spirit."

THEY WROTE ALL of God's Message to Man.

John 16:13, "When he, the Spirit of Truth, is come, he shall guide you into all the truth."

I Timothy 3:16-17, "All scripture is inspired by God and profitable for teaching, for reproof, for correction, for training in righteousness; that the man of God may be adequate, equipped for EVERY good work."

II Peter 1:3, "Seeing that His divine power has granted to us EVERYTHING pertaining to life and godliness, through the true knowledge of Him who called us by His own glory and excellence."

Jude 3, "I felt the necessity to write to you appealing that you contend earnestly for the faith which was ONCE for all delivered to the saints."

THINGS MAN IS FORBIDDEN to do to God's Perfect and Complete Revelation.

I. CAN NOT ADD TO IT

I Corinthians 4:6, "That in us you might learn NOT TO EXCEED what is written."

II John 9, "Any one who GOES TOO FAR and does NOT ABIDE in the teaching of Christ, does not have God; the one who abides in the teaching, he has both the Father and the Son."

Revelation 22:18, "I testify to everyone who hears the words of the prophecy of this book: if anyone ADDS to them, God shall add to him the plagues which are written in this book."

II. CAN NOT SUBTRACT FROM IT

Revelation 22:19, "If anyone TAKES AWAY from the words of the book of this prophecy, God shall take away his part from the tree of life and from the holy city."

III. CAN NOT CHANGE IT

Galatians 1:6-9, "I am amazed that you are so quickly deserting Him who called you by the grace of Christ, for a different gospel; which is really not another; only there are some who are disturbing you, and want to DISTORT the gospel of Christ. But even though we, or an angel from heaven, should preach to you a gospel contrary to that which we have preached to you, let him be accursed. As we have said before, so I say again now, if any man is preaching to you a gospel contrary to that which you received, let him be accursed."

CONCLUSION: THE ABOVE FORBIDS MAN FROM DOING ANYTHING WITH THE BIBLE OTHER THAN TO USE IT AS ABSOLUTE AUTHORITY AND TO OBEY IT.

IX
Scientific Difficulties of the Theory of Evolution

1. INTRODUCTION

While Bible-believing people do object to the teaching of evolution (that life came from non-life; then, from some one-celled life, all the species seen today developed) in that it contradicts the Bible, perhaps as strong a reason for objecting to the teaching of evolution as a "fact" is because it simply is not true to scientific knowledge. The student needs to learn what all leading scientists already know—the theory of evolution has never been proven as a fact. The student also ought to be told that this theory is encumbered with serious difficulties. Yet, many authors who know this still make rash assertions as to the "fact" of evolution.

One high school textbook reads, "All reputable biologists have agreed that evolution of life on earth is an established fact." (*Biology For You*, by B.B. Vance and D. F. Miller, J. B. Lippincott Co., 1950, p. 580.)

Another current textbook being used nationally reads, "Biologists are convinced that the human species evolved from non-human forms . . ." (*Biological Science: Molecule to Man*, Blue Version, Houghton Mifflin Co., Boston, p. 414.)

Many students have come to accept such statements without question. But the truth of the matter is far from what is asserted in the above quotations. Not all scientists, not all biologists, accept the statement that "evolution is a proven fact." For example, Dr. W. R. Thompson, who was for many years Director of the Commonwealth Institute of Biological Control at Ottawa, Canada, and a world-renowned biologist, wrote in his foreword to the 1956 edition of Darwin's *Origin of the Species*, published in the Darwinian Centennial Year as a part of the Everyman's Library Series:

"As we know, there is a great divergence of opinion among biologists, not only about the causes of evolution but even about the actual process. This divergence exists because the evidence is unsatisfactory and does not permit any certain conclusion. It is therefore right and proper to draw the attention of the non-scientific public to the disagreements about evolution. But some recent remarks of evolutionists show that they think this unreasonable. This situation, where men rally to the defense of a doctrine they are unable to defend scientifically, much less demonstrate with scientific rigor, attempting to maintain its credit with the public by the suppression of criticism and the elimination of difficulties, is abnormal and undesirable in science."

Dr. G. A. Kerkut, Professor of Physiology and Biochemistry at the University of Southampton, England, and himself an evolutionist, states:

"This theory . . . can be called the General Theory of Evolution and the evidence that supports it is not sufficiently strong to allow us to consider it as anything more than a working hypothesis . . . the answer (to the problem of evolution) will be found by future experimental work and not by dogmatic assertions that the General Theory of Evolution must be correct because there is nothing else that will satisfactorily take its place." (*The Implications of Evolution*, Pergamon Press, London, 1960, p. 157.)

Kerkut's book caused considerable anguish in the evolutionists' camp. John T. Bonner, a bona fide evolutionist, wrote in review of Kerkut's book:

"This is a book with a disturbing message; it points to some unseemly cracks in the foundation. One is disturbed because what is said gives us the uneasy feeling that we knew it for a long time deep down but were never willing to admit this even to ourselves. It is another one of those cold uncompromising situations where the naked truth and human nature travel in different directions. The particular truth is simply that we have no reliable evidence as to the evolutionary sequence of invertebrate phyla. We do not know whether Protozoa occurred once, or twice, or many times. . . . We have all been telling our students for years not to accept any statement on its face value but to examine the evidence, and therefore, it is rather a shock to discover that we have failed to follow our own sound advice." ("Review of Kerkut's Book," *American Scientist*, Vol. 49, June 1961, p. 240)

These last three quotations indicate clearly that the first two were simply assertions void of virtue or fact. Evolution is not an "established fact" accepted without dispute by scientists. The author or teacher who so states is either ignorant of the facts in the case, or is seeking to hide them from his students. Student—Keep this in mind! There is a "great divergence of opinion among biologists" as to evolution. This is because "the evidence is unsatisfactory and does not permit any certain conclusions."

EXAMINE THE EVIDENCE

Students should follow the advice of the scientist, as suggested by Dr. John T. Bonner, and not accept any statement on its face value, but examine the evidence. Ask questions, point out contradictions, ask for proof when assertions are made. In the following pages certain scientific fields will be examined and pertinent questions asked within those disciplines as to the validity of evolution. These questions bear upon evolution and should be weighed by the teacher and the student in search of scientific truth. The truth-seeker will not seek to avoid difficulties that challenge his theories. Study these questions until you fully understand them and how they relate to evolution in that given field of study. Seek to cause others to see this also. Use textbooks or a dictionary for the definitions in each field of study.

2. ANTHROPOLOGY

QUESTION: Is it possible that the "apelike" skeletons of some of the Neanderthal Men could have been caused by disease?

FACT: (1) Concerning the first Neanderthal skeleton found, in 1908 at La Chapellaux-Saints, and its use as a model in textbooks, it was examined recently by Drs. W. L. Straus and A. J. E. Cave of John Hopkins Medical University, Laboratory of Physical Anthropology and the Department of Anatomy. Their findings were delivered in a symposium commemorating the 50th anniversary of the discovery of the Neanderthal Man. They state there is positive evidence that the first skeleton had osteo-arthritis. "There is nothing about the Neanderthal man that would necessarily cause him to walk differently than ourselves. . . . Yet Neanderthal man with 'arthritis' has been posing for half a century in museums and countless textbooks, illustrating the supposed transition from 'stooped-over' to 'erect'." ("Pathology and the Posture of Neanderthal", *Quarterly Review of Biology*. Dec. 1957, pp. 348-363)

FACT: (2) Some Neanderthal remains are an excellent parallel to the modern description of Acromegaly, a chronic disease characterized by bone thickening of adults. As one medical text book describes it, it eventually causes "apelike features" (see any medical book for a description of this bone growth disorder). People today with this disease (1 in 10,000) have skeletons comparable to those of the Neanderthal. As evidence it was a disease among some adult types, "the remains of young Neanderthal children (such as the Gibralter Neanderthal Child) appear as children would today, showing no signs of this bone disorder which gave an 'apelike' appearance to adults." (Cromwell, *The Making of Man*, Phoenix House Ltd., London, p. 55)

QUESTION: Can the Neanderthal Man be classed as modern in stature?

FACT: (1) "There is no valid reason for the assumption that the posture of Neanderthal Man of the fourth glacial period differed significantly from that of the present-day man." (Drs. W. L. Straus and A. J. E. Cave, previously cited)

FACT: (2) All of its features fall within the range of variation found in modern man. (Same as above)

FACT: (3) "The time has come to reappraise one of the most foully slandered creatures ever to walk the

earth—the Neanderthal man. . . . Shaved and barbered
and dressed in a modern suit of clothes, Neanderthal
Man would probably attract little attention in a crowd
at a football game" (Daniel Cohen, *Science Digest.* Oct.
1968, pp. 13-18).

*QUESTION: Do scientists consider the Java Man casts
or illustrations to be accurate?*

FACT: (1) The Java Man is a portrait of a thigh bone,
of a few teeth, and a fragment of a cranium. These were
found along a river bank, making it impossible to tell
their origin. Found near them were two very large
skulls (Wadjak skulls) which Dr. E. Dubois kept hidden
for twenty-five years. The Wadjak skulls are now
discredited for being "of vague geology." Why not the
Java Man fossils found with them which were held from
view in Dr. E. Dubois' closet for over twenty-five
years? Note: "None of the published illustrations or
casts now in various museums are accurate. The jaw
fragment was from another and later type man. The
femur is without doubt human" (Dr. Hrdlika, "Skeleton
In a Closet," *Science*, June 15, 1923).

*QUESTION: Is the stated antiquity of the Heidelberg
Man accepted without question by all scientists?*

FACT: (1) "Massive jawbones, resembling in many
details of structure the jaw of the ancient Heidelberg
man, have been found by professor E. H. Burhitt of
Sidney University, in a collection of modern human
remains from the South Sea Island of New Caledonia.
. . . But the natives of New Caledonia are not
lowbrows; even though they are savages, the skulls are
'modern' and their brains are just about as large as
those of contemporary Europeans" (*Science*, Oct. 26,
1928, p. 124). The skulls of these natives have massive

jawbones almost identical with the Heidelberg Jaw, yet they do not have "ape-like" heads. Why should one then accept the necessity of such from a single fossil jaw when we have living specimens to the contrary?

FACT: (2) This fossil jaw, from which the Heidelberg man was created, was found in Heidelberg 80 feet below the surface. As no implements or fossils have been found in the deposit that held the jaw, it is not possible to date it even approximately. Because the jaw was so big some gave it an early date, which date seems to remain.

QUESTION: Have not "modern" human remains been found fossilized in ancient strata?

FACT: (1) Human remains of a modern man, woman, and two children were found at Castenedolo, Italy, by Professor Ragazzoni. These were found while digging for molluscs in a Pliocene strata (15 million years old*). "As the student of prehistoric man reads and studies the records of the 'Castenedolo' find, a feeling of incredulity rises within him. He cannot reject the discovery as false without doing injury to his sense of truth, and he cannot accept it without shattering his accepted beliefs. It is clear that we cannot pass Castenedolo by in silence: all the modern problems relating to the origin and antiquity of modern man focus themselves around it" (Sir Arthur Keith, *The Antiquity of Man*, p. 119).

FACT: (2) The Calaveras Skull found in Calaveras County, California. It was taken from a tunnel dug 150 feet below the surface, of which 100 feet was solid Sierra lava flow, along with man made stone implements and some extinct fossils of the early Pliocene strata (15 million years old*) (Professor

*Dated by evolutionists.

101

Wright's article in *The Century*, Apr. 1891). As Professor W. H. Holmes put it: "To suppose that man could have remained unchanged physically, mentally, socially, industrially and aesthetically for a million years, roughly speaking (and all this implied by the evidence furnished), seems in the present state of our knowledge hardly less than admitting a miracle." (quoted from Dr. Douglas Dewar, *The Transformist Illusion*, Dehoff Pub., Murfreesboro, Tenn.)

FACT: (3) The many fossil human footprints found in supposedly old formations. Among them the pair of human sandal prints found at Antelope Springs in Utah (1969) in Cambrian rock (400 million years old*) along with fossil trilobites, one in the heel of the left print. Another is the several dozen human footprints found among Dinosaur prints along the Paluxy River, Glen Rose, Texas. Both are in Cretaceous rock (about 100 million years old*).

FACT: (4) "The *Western* European classic Neanderthal type was altogether a too complete answer to Darwinian prayer. . . . Heretical and non-conforming fossil men were banished to the limbo of dark museum cupboards, forgotten or even destroyed" (Prof. E. A. Hooten, *Apes, Men, and Morons*, 1938, p. 107).

*Dated by evolutionists.

3. PALEONTOLOGY

QUESTION: Do paleontologists agree that the fossil record substantiates the theory of evolution?

FACT: (1) "The sudden emergence of major adaptive types, as seen in the abrupt appearance in the fossil record of families and orders, continue to give trouble. The phenomena lay in the genetical no man's land beyond the limits of experimentation. A few paleontologists even today cling to the idea that these gaps will be closed by further collecting, i.e. that they are accidents of sampling; but most regard the observed discontinuities as real, and have sought an explanation for them." (D. Dwight Davis, *Genetics, Paleontology, and Evolution*, Princeton University Press 1949, p. 74.)

FACT: (2) "No matter how far back we go in the fossil records of previous animal life upon the earth we find no trace of any animal forms which are intermediate between various major groups or phyla. . . . The greatest groups of animal life do not merge into one another. They are and have been fixed from the beginning. . . . No animals are known even from the earliest rocks which cannot at once be assigned to their proper phylum or major group." (Dr. A. H. Clark, *The New Evolution, Zoogenesis*, Williams and Wilkins, Baltimore, 1930, p. 189.)

FACT: (3) "So we see that the fossil record, the actual history of the animal life on earth, bears out the assumption that at its very first appearance animal life in its broader features was essentially the same as that which we now know it. . . . Thus, so far as concerns the major groups of animals, the creationists seem to have the better of the argument. There is not the slightest evidence that any of the major groups arose from any other" (Dr. A. H. Clark, *Quarterly Review of Biology*, Dec. 1928, p. 539).

FACT: (4) Charles Darwin wrote: "Long before the reader has arrived at this part of my work, a crowd of difficulties will have occurred to him. . . . Why, if species have descended from other species by fine graduations, do we not everywhere see innummerable transitional forms? Why is not all nature in confusion, instead of the species being, as we see them, well defined?" (Darwin, *The Origin of the Species*, chap. 6, first page).

FACT: (5) "The facts are that many species and genera, indeed the majority, do appear suddenly in the record, differing sharply and in many ways from any earlier groups, and that this appearance of discontinuity becomes more common the higher the level, until it is virtually universal as regards orders and all higher steps in the taxonomic hierarchy. This essentially paleontological problem is also of crucial interest for all other biologists, and since there is such a conflict of opinion, non-paleontologists may choose either to believe the authority who agrees with their prejudices, or to discard the evidence as worthless" (George Gaylord Simpson, *Temp and Mode in Evolution*, Columbia Press, 1944, p. 99). Discussing the lack of fossil evidence for transitional forms leading up to the 32 orders of mammals, Dr. Simpson says, "This regular absence of transitional forms is not confined to mammals, but is an almost universal phenomenon, as has long been noted by paleontologists" (G. G. Simpson, *Temp and Mode of Evolution*, Columbia University Press, New York, 1944, p. 106).

QUESTION: Does the Pre-Cambrian strata contain evidence of any form of life leading up to and into the Cambrian era, which contains over 5000 species of animals?

FACT: (1) Darwin wrote: "To the question why we do not find rich fossiliferous deposits belonging to these assumed earliest periods prior to the Cambrian system,

I can give no satisfactory answer. . . . I look at the geological record as a history of the world imperfectly kept. . . . Nevertheless, the difficulty of assigning any good reason for the absence of vast piles of strata rich in fossils beneath the Cambrian system is very great" (Darwin, *The Origin of the Species*, chap. 10).

FACT: (2) "Fossils are abundant only from the Cambrian onward. . . . Darwin was aware of this problem, even more striking in his day than in ours, when it is still striking enough. He said of it: 'the case at present must remain inexplicable; and may be truly urged as a valid argument against the views here entertained' (Darwin, Chapter X). Darwin's case is still not clearly explained with sufficient positive evidence" (George Gaylord Simpson, "The History of Life", in *Evolution After Darwin*, Vol. 1, *The Evolution of Life*, U. of Chicago Press, 1960, p. 143).

FACT: (3) "Fossils would provide the only direct evidence of the earliest living things, but none have been found, and it is improbable that any exist in a form still recognizable" (Simpson, "Biological Sciences," *The Great Ideas of Today Yearbook*, 1965, Encyclopedia Britannica, Inc. Chicago, p. 292). This statement was made by one of the world's leading paleontologists and authority on evolution. Dr. Simpson, deeply disturbed by the absence of pre-Cambrian fossils, called it "the major mystery of the history of life" (George Gaylord Simpson, *The Meaning of Evolution*, Yale University Press, New Haven, 1949).

FACT: (4) "Molecular and organismal biologists are now beginning a cooperation that will surely prove fruitful. Numerous efforts have been initiated in the last year or so to interpret molecular biology in evolutionary terms. It is too early to say just what the results will be, but they are certainly promising" (Same as above, p. 315).

Note: George Gaylord Simpson is a paleontologist now at Harvard University, and formerly professor of Vertebrate Paleontology at Columbia University. Before that he was Curator of Fossil Mammals and Birds at the American Museum of Natural History in New York City. He is a world-renowned paleontologist, and ardent evolutionist, and yet in 1965 he admits the fossil record does not prove evolution and refers us to the field of biology, hopeful it will soon bear fruit to prove evolution. Simpson even returns to the disproved theory of spontaneous generation hoping to save his theory, saying, "The spontaneous generation of the first living things did occur" (Same as above, p. 294). What proof did he offer? None! Just an empty assertion!

Isn't it strange indeed that evolutionary scientists leave their own field and point the student to another for the "proof" of the theory of evolution?

FACT: (5) Modern type pine pollen (a conifer spore) has been recently found in Hakati Shale, Pre-Cambrian rock, in the Grand Canyon by Dr. Clifford Burdick using the facilities of the University of Arizona. This appears, to date, to be the only positive plant or animal life in the Pre-Cambrian era, yet it is one of the most modern plant types on the evolutionist's time scale.

Note: This evidence is devastating to the theory of evolution—the fossil records *do not* indicate that any one kind of plant or animal ever changed into another. Paleontologists know this, and state it. Teachers should do the same.

4. COMPARATIVE ANATOMY

QUESTION: Are scientists in the field of Comparative Anatomy agreed that there exists a known evolutionary scale indicating which animals evolved from which animals?

FACT: (1) "The all-too-frequent picture of evolution as a progression from amoeba to man, is, and always has been, utterly without foundation" (Prof. Paul Weisz, *The Science of Biology*, McGraw Hill Book Co., 1959, p. 655).

FACT: (2) "The known presence of parallelisms (similarities of structure in different animal groups) in so many cases and its suspected presence in others suggests that it may have been an almost universal phenomenon. A close student of the subject may, if pressed, be driven to the logical though absurd admission of the possibility that two animals as closely related as, for example, chimpanzee and gorilla, may have evolved in parallel fashion all the way from a piscine stage (ancestral fish)." This is said by Alfred S. Romer, the famous comparative anatomist of Harvard University (Jepsen, *Genetics, Paleontology, and Evolution*, Princeton University Press, 1949, p. 115).

FACT: (3) Professor Hooton of Harvard said, "I am convinced that a zoological classificationist may be as dissolute and irresponsible as a lightning-rod salesman" (Hooton, *Apes, Men, and Morons*, p. 115).

FACT: (4) Because the "evolutionary tree" is constantly being altered, Professor Weidenreich, the famous anthropologist of the University of Chicago, commented, "Unfortunately, there is no objective guage which can be used for measurement of the grade of morphological deviations and for the determination of the limits between individual, specific, and generic variants. Such a distinction is left entirely to the 'opinions of naturalists having sound judgment and wide experiences,' as Darwin put it" (Weidenreich, previously cited, p. 2).

FACT: (5) Paul Weatherwax, Professor of Botany at Indiana University, said, "Botanists still disagree widely on the proper grouping of many plants, but this is because they do not agree in their theories as to the origin of the differences which separate the groups" (Weatherwax, *Plant Biology*, W. B. Saunders Co., 1942, p. 240).

QUESTION: Do the various displays of the supposed evolved horse have difficulties and contradictions in the models?

FACT: (1) The anatomy of the various models does not compare. For example, the rib count varies back and forth from 15 to 19, and the lumbars of the backbone vary back and forth from 6 to 8. Many eminent scientists disagree on which is the theoretical chain of fossil horses, as selected from the over 250 available specimens.

FACT: (2) Some of these skeleton structures are significantly larger than their supposed descendants.

FACT: (3) ". . . at present, however, it is a matter of faith that the textbook pictures are true, or even that they are the best representations of the truth that are available to us at the present time" (Kerkut, *Implications of Evolution*, Pergamon Press, 1960, p. 148).

FACT: (4) The American Museum of Natural History,

New York City, describes the difference between the "Dawn Horse" (first) and the Equus (modern) in their *Guide Leaflet Series 36*: "The proportion of the skull, the short neck, and arched back, and the limbs of moderate length, were very little horse-like, recalling on the contrary, some modern carnivorous animals, especially the Civets (cats)."

Many scientists have concluded that the Hyrax living in Africa is the descendant of the Eohippus ("Dawn Horse"). The similarity is extremely striking. Both are the size of a rabbit, live in thickets, appear to have the same lifestyle, have four toes on the fore limbs and three toes on the hind limbs.

FACT: (5) Two recently discovered remains of horses (Equus Nevadenis and Equus Occidentalis) are identical to today's horses (Equus). These two species appear with the saber-tooth tiger, who is also known to be contemporary with the "Dawn Horse" (supposed first). Real horses appeared in full bloom during the Oligocene Age (supposedly 30 million years ago) (Frank W. Cousin's, *The Alleged Evolution of The Horse*, Symposium on Creation III, Baker Book House, 1971).

Note: Present day paleontologists are aware that not only does a living copy of the supposed "dawn horse" exist today, but that full size fossil remains of "modern horse" has been found in supposed ancient strata where his presumed small ancestors were to have begun his evolution.

QUESTION: Do not evolutionists teach that descendant species tend to become more complex and increase in size?

FACT: (1) Fossils reveal dragon flies just as they are today except much larger, some having an 18 inch wingspread; sloths weighing 4 tons; etc.

FACT: (2) Many living species of seashell life can be found which are in the fossil record. They have not changed from the earliest life of the Cambrian time.

5. BIOLOGY

QUESTION: Do biologists teach transmutation [mutations causing new groups of animals] as a scientific fact?

FACT: (1) All biology textbooks teach that there is no laboratory or other proof that transmutations can be true. Mendal's Law of Heredity is accepted by biologists as a scientific truth—"Like begets like" with variations caused by breeding or mutations which are the result of different heredity or physical alterations within the original species. Biologists know that scientists can classify animals into species on a basis of the chromosomes contained within the organism.

FACT: (2) All scientists recognize "micro-evolution" as caused by mutations within a family of plants or animals. It is "mega-evolution," proving one family "evolved" via transmutations into another, that has defied proof.

QUESTION: Do biologists believe the Law of Biogenesis can be disproved?

FACT: (1) Biologists do believe the Law of Biogenesis—("Life begets Life")—was proved by Louis Pasteur's Swan-neck Flask Experiment, 1860, which refuted the theory of spontaneous generation, and was called a victory for the biologists. Current biology textbooks teach the law as accepted, for none has been able to disprove it. According to the most modern science, life does not originate from non-living material.

QUESTION: Why do biologists who believe in evolution point students to the fields of paleontology and comparative anatomy for the "proof" of their theory?

FACT: (1) "Biologists are convinced that the human species evolved from non-human forms. They base their conclusions on the fossils of primates, and on comparisons of human structures and functions with those of other living primates" (The Blue Version, already cited, p. 414).

Note: The study of the "fossils of Primates" is in the field of Paleontology; the "comparison of human structures" is in the discipline of Comparative Anatomy. Why are biologists going over to those fields to draw their conclusions? This is a tacit admission that no proof lies in the field of Biology for the theory of evolution, and we have already seen that Paleontologists and Comparative Anatomists deny they have the solid evidence for the theory. In fact, they believe the hope of its proof lies with the biologists—in molecular biology as previously noted.

QUESTION: Why do biologists rely on mutations to be the mechanism of evolution?

FACT: (1) "The process of mutation is the only known source of new materials of genetic variability, and hence evolution." This and the following statements were said by Professor Dobzhansky, one of the outstanding geneticists of today (Sinnot, Dunn, and Dobzhansky, *Principles of Genetics*, 4th ed., Macmillan. 1950, p. 315).

FACT: (2) "Most mutations which arise in any organism are more or less disadvantageous to their possessors. The classical mutants obtained in Drosophila (fruit fly) usually show deterioration, breakdown, and the disappearance of some organs" (Dobzhansky, Theodosius, *Evolution, Genetics, and Man*, Wiley and Sons, 1955, p. 105).

FACT: (3) "The deleterious character of most mutations seems to be a very serious difficulty" (*Evolution, Genetics, and Man*, cited above, p. 105).

FACT: (4) Dr. L. B. Dunn, Professor of Zoology at Columbia University, says "Such events, known as mutations, are the ultimate source of the hereditary variety characteristic of all species. It is this variety upon which the natural selection and other evolutionary forces act in forming varieties, races, species, and other natural categories" (Dunn, *Heredity and Evolution in Human Populations*, Harvard Press, 1959, p. 7).

QUESTION: Do mutations make new structures and organs?

FACT: (1) Mutations are known to cause only one of the following genetic alterations in a living structure: (1) Complete removal of the structure; (2) relocation of the structure; (3) an abnormal multiplication of the structure; (4) and a varying of the size or coloring of the structure. Mutations only vary existing genes; they do not create new genes. Therefore they are not a source for adding a new structure to any living plant or animal. "In cases of homeosis in which a single gene may, as in the fruit fly (Drosophila melanogaster), replace antennae by legs, certain mouthparts by legs, balancers by wings, etc., the gene is to be looked upon not as a germinal representative of the whole complex structure but as a switch which alters conditions so as to set going a long established reaction system in a strange location" (Wright, Sewell, *Encyclopedia Britan-*

nica, "Evolution," 1957).

FACT: (2) Dr. Hooton of Harvard, "Saltatory evolution by way of mutation, is a very convenient way of bridging over gaps between animal forms. . . . Now I am afraid that many anthropologists (including myself) have sinned against genetic science and are leaning upon a broken reed when we depend upon mutations" (*Apes, Men, and Morons,* previously cited, p. 118).

6. PHYSICS

QUESTION: Since the radiocarbon (C-14) method of dating is based on the assumption that the amount of C-14 in the atmosphere has been constant, has it been proven to be constant?

FACT: (1) "Radiocarbon dating is based on the incorrect assumption that C-14 is in equilibrium, the rate of formation equaling the rate of decay. But recent data show the rate of formation is 18.4 and the rate of decay 13.3 so that a non-equilibrium condition exists. This situation telescopes all radiocarbon ages to about 10,000 years or less. . . . In analyzing this equilibrium postulate, Libby, the author of the radiocarbon method, himself found evidence for this unbalance. However, he discounted the evidence for this unbalance in favor of what he took to be more compelling, albeit hearsay, evidence that the earth is too old for C-14 to be out of balance. . . . Libby found the rate of decay to be 15.3 counts per gram per minute for carbon from the living biosphere, and the rate of formation to be 18.8" (Dr. Melvin Cook, Professor of Metallurgy at the University of Utah, "Radiological Dating and Some Pertinent Applications", *Creation Research Society Quarterly,* Sept. 1968, Ann Arbor, Mich. p. 69).

FACT: (2) The laboratory at UCLA which is under the direction of Dr. Libby issued this statement, "It has been shown on the basis of these investigations that variations from the assumed initial activity of some of these samples do exist. Recent elaborate studies have now demonstrated conclusively that the initial activity of C-14 samples and thus the rate of C-14 production has varied with time. Most recently, the work of Suess (1965, J. Geophys. Res., V. 70, p. 5937;5952) has clearly pointed out these variations" ("On the Accuracy of Radiocarbon Dates," *Geochronicle*, UCLA, Vol. 2, No. 2, June 1966).

QUESTION: Can bones be dated directly by the C-14 process?

FACT: (1) "We have had no experience with bone as such and believe that it is a very poor prospect for two reasons; the carbon content of a bone is extremely low, being largely in inorganic form in a very porous structure; and it is extremely likely to have suffered alteration" (Willard F. Libby, *Radiocarbon Dating*, University of Chicago Press, 1955, p. 45).

QUESTION: Have the "radioactive clocks" been proven accurate in telling the earth's age?

FACT: (1) Recent research upon young rocks of known age challenges this assumption. Isotopic ratios (elements resulting from radioactive decay) indicate that even "young" volcanic deposits are at an advanced stage of decay, giving theoretical "ages" of thousands of millions of years. Attempts to check the reliability of radioactive dating by the potassium-argon method has been carried out by the University of Hawaii on island volcanic rocks. It was reported that "excess argon" caused volcanic rock (formed within the last two hundred years) to have an apparent age of hundreds of millions of years. In the case of previously calculated ages, where the real ages were unknown though presumed to be old, this excess argon was not noticed. But in the case of rocks known to be young, it was very obvious that the ages calculated had no relationship to the real ages (Funkhouser, Barnes, and Haughton, "The problems of dating volcanic rocks by the potassium-argon method. Bull. Volcan., 29:709., 1966).

FACT: (2) Research by the Academy of Science USSR has been carried out on eighteen samples from twelve volcanoes containing radioactive materials in the Uranium 238 series. It was found that isotopes in the chain were in disequilibrium. The ratios between the daughter elements in the Uranium 238 series were found to be far greater than can be accounted for through the normal process of decay, indicating that some isotope material must have been present in the mineral bodies at the time of their genesis. Since the dating of mineral bodies is done by measuring the ratios between these isotopes, and it is known that an unmeasurable quantity of isotopes did not form by decay from Uranium, it is pure speculation to guess at the original amount of isotope material, and thereby produce a ratio to get a date of origin. These samples were taken from volcanic flow known to have occurred within the last 200 years, yet the "radioactive clock" dating gave them an age in the 100's of millions of years (Cherdyntsev, Kislisina and Zverev, Isotopic composition of uranium and thorium in rocks and products of active volcanism., Geological Institute, Academy of Sciences, U.S.S.R., Earth Science Section, 172:178).

FACT: (3) Studies using the Uranium decay series in the U.S. on ten recently active volcanoes were expected to give very small ratios due to their young age. Instead the ratios were extremely large indicating from 5,000 million to 10,500 million years of age (Sidney P. Clementson, "A Critical Examination Of Radioactive Dating Of Rock," *Creation Research Quarterly*, Dec. 1970, p. 137).

FACT: (4) "In addition to knowing the rate of formation of decay products and the present amount of them, it is also necessary to know the original amount of them before decay started. It is not sufficient to just assume zero amounts of material. In most cases the decay products are just like materials already naturally present in the sample even when no radioactive decay has occurred. In other words, we are back to the problem of knowing the original conditions. In the case of the age of the earth, it is obvious that no scientist made records of the initial condition" (Dr. Donald Chittick, "Dating the Earth and Fossils," George Fox College, 1968).

The conclusion which can be drawn from these facts, which applies equally to dating of all mineral bearing rocks, is that calculated ages give no indication whatever of the ages of the host rocks. These ages have no relationship to the age of the earth, because the various ages computed have varied so widely. Consequently ratios of parent and daughter elements are merely ratios, and their use as a base for projecting "ages" of the rocks, or of the earth itself, is highly questionable and fraught with many assumptions that cannot be checked.

QUESTION: Can radioactive materials that cause "halos" in igneous rock, discount the theory of the slow evolution of the earth?

FACT: (1) "The half-life of polonium 214 is only 164 microseconds. According to one theory of the planet's origin, the earth cooled down from a hot gaseous mass and gradually solidified over a period of hundreds of millions of years. If this were so, polonium halos could not possibly have formed because all the polonium would have decayed soon after it was synthesized and would have been extinct when the crustal rocks formed. . . . Unless the creation of the radioactivity and rocks were simultaneous there would be no picture—no variant pleochroic halos. Further, by virtue of the very short half-life, the radioactivity and formation of the rocks must be almost instantaneous" (Dr. Robert V. Gentry, "Cosmology and Earth's Invisible Realm," *Medical Opinion and Review*, Oct. 1967, p. 65-79).

QUESTION: Do the laws of physics harmonize or conflict with the theory of evolution?

FACT: (1) The creation of the physical universe must have preceded the First Law of Thermodynamics (matter and energy can be neither created nor destroyed, only interchanged).

FACT: (2) Then—the creation of life on this earth must have preceded the Law of Biogenesis (Life begets life).

FACT: (3) After which—the creation of the physical universe and the life on the earth—a fully woundup biophysical world preceded the Second Law of Thermodynamics (The universe is running down as a watch—the universe's sum of total usable energy is constantly decreasing).

THEREFORE: This postulates a *Special Creation* which is unexplainable by modern science. *Both* the Evolutionists and the Creationists believe in a *Special Creation!!*

—THIS PRESENTS ONE OF TWO CHOICES—

1. Life, intelligence, order, and energy buildup came from inert dead matter or nothing. Not compatible with modern science or the concept of God.
2. Life, intelligence, order, and energy buildup, and matter came from that which had Life, Total Power, and Intelligence. *Compatible With Modern Science And The Concept Of God!*

FACT: "Turn away from the profane babblings and oppositions of science—which is falsely so called; which some professing have erred concerning the faith." (Apostle Paul, 1 Timothy 6:20).